Internal Control/
Anti-Fraud Program
Design for the Small Business

The Wiley Corporate F&A series provides information, tools, and insights to corporate professionals responsible for issues affecting the profitability of their company, from accounting and finance to internal controls and performance management.

Founded in 1807, John Wiley & Sons is the oldest independent publishing company in the United States. With offices in North America, Europe, Asia, and Australia, Wiley is globally committed to developing and marketing print and electronic products and services for our customers' professional and personal knowledge and understanding.

Internal Control/ Anti-Fraud Program Design for the Small Business

A Guide for Companies NOT Subject to the Sarbanes-Oxley Act

STEVE DAWSON

WILEY

For general information on our other products and services or for technical support, please contact our Customer Care Department within the United States at (800) 762-2974, outside the United States at (317) 572-3993 or fax (317) 572-4002.

Wiley publishes in a variety of print and electronic formats and by print-on-demand. Some material included with standard print versions of this book may not be included in e-books or in print-on-demand. If this book refers to media such as a CD or DVD that is not included in the version you purchased, you may download this material at http://booksupport.wiley.com. For more information about Wiley products, visit www.wiley.com.

Library of Congress Cataloging-in-Publication Data:

Dawson, Steve, 1962–
    Internal control/anti-fraud program for the small private business : a guide for companies not subject to the Sarbanes-Oxley Act / Steve Dawson.
        pages cm. — (Wiley corporate F&A series)
    Includes index.
    ISBN 978-1-119-06507-4 (hardback); ISBN 978-1-119-08372-6 (ePDF);
ISBN 978-1-119-08371-9 (ePub); ISBN 978-1-119-08373-3 (obook)
    1. Fraud—United States—Prevention.   2. Small business—United States—Auditing.   I. Title.
    HV6691.D39 2015
    658.4'73—dc23

                                                                    2014049431
Printed in the United States of America
10 9 8 7 6 5 4 3 2 1

To my wonderful wife, Ebeth, the matriarch of our incredible family and the strongest person I have ever known. Without your constant support, this work would have never become a reality.

Contents

 PART I: THE ANTI-FRAUD ENVIRONMENT: THE BLUEPRINTS, THE FOUNDATION, THE GROUND FLOOR

Preface: Maybe It's Time We Get Back to the Basics

L ARRY WAS THE CHIEF FINANCIAL OFFICER for a company with annual revenues of $75 million. He worked his way up through the company over a period of 10 years to attain this prestigious position. Unfortunately, external financial pressures in his life led him down the path of compromise and ultimately to prison. As his struggles intensified, Larry rationalized that he would only "borrow" the money from the company; he would, of course, pay it back once he got past these financial pressures. "I'm not committing fraud. I'm not stealing. I'm just borrowing," he constantly told himself. Since Larry had risen through the ranks over a long period, his superiors trusted him. Because of their level of trust, Larry was virtually unaccountable to the system of checks and balances that existed over the disbursement process. By the time the fraud was discovered, Larry had misappropriated over $1.3 million from his employer through a simple disbursement fraud scheme.

Larry's story is true. It is based on only one of my numerous experiences investigating fraud cases over the span of 30 years. Sadly, this same story occurs often in today's business environment. Fraud has become too easy, too frequent, and too costly for the small business community. If we consider the fact that in the United States fraud costs approximately $5 to $6 billion annually, we begin to understand that occupational fraud, or internal fraud, is not a small problem. So what can we do to reduce these occurrences? We must install a properly designed, properly functioning anti-fraud program specifically tailored to every individual company that exists. This is not a new concept. However, just because we possess the knowledge that something needs to be done doesn't mean we are doing it. In fact, my experiences indicate that it isn't being done at all.

ANTI-FRAUD PROGRAM DESIGN FOR THE SMALL BUSINESS

"I know I need better internal controls. I just don't know how to go about it." For the past 30 years, I have heard board members, chief executives, accountants, and other employees utter this statement. In most cases, this occurs right after fraud has already been committed within their company.

The guidance in this book is directed to the small business community, specifically to those businesses not subject to the complex provisions of the Sarbanes-Oxley Act. Anti-fraud program design issues for small businesses are unique, with their own problems to consider. For example, small businesses most likely don't have 25 people in their accounting departments to naturally create a segregation of duties that helps deter fraud. A small business requires additional procedures to prevent fraud from occurring within departments comprised of very few people. Thus the purpose of this book is to address these issues in the small business community. So who or what is considered a small business?

 ## SMALL BUSINESS DEFINED

What is the literal definition of a small business? Is it the mom-and-pop grocery store around the corner? The not-for-profit organization providing services in your community? Perhaps the local bank or credit union, your city or county government, or even the manufacturing plant just outside of town? If you spend any time researching the definition of a small business, you will see quickly that the term *small business* is defined according to various parameters: total assets, total revenue, number of employees, or a combination of two or all of these factors.

The U.S. Small Business Administration (SBA) defines a small business as "one that is independently owned and operated, is organized for profit, and is not dominant in its field."[1] For size standards, the SBA classifies the business into specific industries and then applies the criteria of number of employees or annual receipts. In fact, a business can have up to 1,500 employees and be considered a small business. This definition excludes the not-for-profit organizations, city and county governments, and school districts, just to name a few. While not specifically defining a small business, the National Federation of Independent Business (NFIB) states that its membership spans the spectrum of business operations ranging from sole proprietors to firms with hundreds of employees. According to the NFIB, the typical member employs 10 people and reports gross sales of about $500,000 annually.[2] U.S. Census Bureau information indicates that

---

[1] The definition was taken from the Small Business Administration website at www.sba.gov/content/what-sbas-definition-small-business-concern.

[2] This information is from the NFIB's website at www.nfib.com/about-nfib/what-is-nfib/who-nfib-represents.

employers with fewer than 500 employees account for as much as 99 percent of our nation's businesses. In considering all of this information, the one fact that becomes clear is that there is no agreed-upon standard definition for what qualifies as a small business.

Given these definitions and the variety of criteria used to formulate them, I submit that the term *small business* can refer to any business, from the mom-and-pop grocery store to the manufacturing plant just outside of town.

The Public Company versus the Nonpublic (Private) Company

Given this general understanding of the definition of a small business, we can then further classify our nation's businesses into two categories: public companies and nonpublic (private) companies. The technical aspects of the definitions of each category are somewhat mind-numbing and do not represent the focus of this book; therefore, I will spare you the details. Generally, a public company is one whose stock is traded on an open stock exchange or over the counter in the stock market and has financial accountability to the stockholders and to the U.S. Securities and Exchange Commission. The nonpublic company does not have the same nature of accountability as generally defined for public companies.

Why the Distinction?

Consider that you are the owner, a board member, or a management employee of a small business not classified as a public company. Whether you have one or a thousand employees, you can, and most likely will, experience internal fraud in your company. Internal fraud is fraud that is perpetrated against the company by an employee or in collusion between an employee and an external party. Because the risk of fraud exists in any company of any size, the need for an effective and efficient anti-fraud program also exists.

We Get It; We Need to Try to Prevent Fraud—So How Do We Do This?

Since the passage of the Sarbanes-Oxley Act (SOX) in 2002 and the resulting creation of the Public Company Accounting Oversight Board, public companies have had the benefit of volumes of information about internal controls and anti-fraud program design. SOX and its requirements are detailed and, unfortunately, complex. As a small business owner myself, I can get overwhelmed quickly when considering all of this information and guidance. The complexity of SOX can frustrate even the savviest small business owner.

It is my belief that the problems associated with how to design an effective and efficient small business anti-fraud program are unique. Even small businesses with just one employee can implement certain practices to accomplish an effective program. SOX really doesn't address these issues for small businesses. It really shouldn't have to; that is not its purpose. What we need is a practical guide for the design of an anti-fraud program with all of the complexity of SOX stripped away. What we need is something we will refer to as *simple practicality.*

Maybe it's time we get back to the basics. Maybe it's time we get back to the commonsense aspects of running our businesses and protecting our assets.

Accordingly, the focus of this book is to provide information regarding the design of an effective and efficient anti-fraud program for the company or business that is not subject to the Sarbanes-Oxley Act.

 ## THE ANTI-FRAUD PROGRAM STRUCTURE

As we discuss designing an anti-fraud program unique to your small business, imagine the familiar metaphor of building a structure—a house in this example. We are going to *build* an effective and efficient anti-fraud program step by step using a commonsense blueprint. Remember, *simple practicality.*

Any reliable building process begins with the architect's blueprints, laying the foundation and the floor, which we will cover in Chapters 1 through 5. Specifically, these chapters address the issues of the anti-fraud environment and the fraud risk assessment process.

Chapters 6 through 9 represent the process of raising the walls and building on the properly laid foundation. These chapters provide specific control activities that can be implemented to safeguard company assets.

Chapters 10 and 11 represent the process of installing the ceiling. Chapter 10 addresses the steps necessary for the proper documentation of the anti-fraud program, and Chapter 11 addresses the issue of communication (a company-wide anti-fraud training program) for the workforce that includes specific training regarding the contents of the anti-fraud program.

Chapter 12 represents the routine maintenance of the expertly finished structure. Once completed, every structure needs to be repaired, repainted, rewired, and so on, from time to time. In this chapter, we address the issues associated with monitoring your business for compliance with the anti-fraud program, along with assessing the effectiveness and efficiency of the program. An anti-fraud program is not a static program; it is a program that changes as operational aspects of the business change. Without proper monitoring of the program, you will have no idea of where to direct routine maintenance.

What could be an incredibly daunting, complicated process in the life of your business is now simply outlined, as a blueprint outlines instructions for building a home. Upon implementation of the guidance presented, you will have a sound, well-thought-out anti-fraud program specifically tailored to your needs. You can be confident in the protection you will put in place for yourself, your employees, and your small business.

Let's begin!

Acknowledgments

COLLABORATION—that is the only word I can use to describe how this work was completed. Because so many have contributed in various ways over the span of 30 years, I can only apologize in advance to anyone I forgot to mention.

I am deeply grateful to my business associate Jeff Smith, who believed in this project and who reviewed the content countless times to ensure that what he knew I wanted to say actually made it to paper.

To Meagan Smith, my manuscript editor, I express appreciation beyond what words can describe. The countless hours of reading, editing, rereading the edits—all with the goal of making the manuscript understandable—will not soon be forgotten.

To my former partners at Bolinger, Segars, Gilbert & Moss—Orland Gilbert, Jack Moss, Barbee Word, Bob Beam, Robert Cobb, Wade Wilson, Greg Gilbert, Tim Baugh, Nathan Paden, Randy Robbins, Bill Miller, and Jeff Marshall—I will forever be grateful for your part in raising me from a young college student in an atmosphere of learning and encouragement. The experiences presented in this work form the legacy of our 26 years together.

Finally, I would like to give a special thank-you to my executive editor, Sheck Cho, and my senior development editor, Stacey Rivera, at John Wiley & Sons for guiding me through the processes of the publishing business and bringing this project to completion.

PART ONE

The Anti-Fraud Environment: The Blueprints, the Foundation, the Ground Floor

REMEMBER VIVIDLY THE EXPERIENCE OF BUILDING my own home. I still remember the dinner with my wife where we crouched over napkins, illustrating each detail of our dreams. As we left the restaurant, we blissfully knew that this was a great idea. Little did we know that our dream home construction would turn into the single most frustrating process of our lives.

Early in the process, after having looked through what seemed like hundreds of magazines and catalogues, we selected what we wanted for items such as faucets, cabinet hardware, and lighting fixtures. Yes, we had finished out our new home. Then it dawned on us that we had not even started the process of finding the architect or a home building contractor. Stepping back for a moment, we realized that some things have to come first, mainly all of the foundational work.

Similar to building a home, the construction of an effective anti-fraud program includes certain issues that must be addressed in the proper order.

First, there must be a plan; a framework must be designed, similar to an architect's blueprint for building a home.

Second, the foundation must be put in place on which to build the structure. Accordingly, certain foundational policies must exist to support the structure of an anti-fraud program.

Once the plan is in place and the foundation is down, the ground floor is ready to be installed. The ground floor, the fraud risk assessment process, is necessary to move forward.

Chapters 1 through 5 address all of these issues that, when approached in the correct order, will result in a reliable anti-fraud environment.

CHAPTER ONE

The Architect's Blueprint

Establishing the Framework

I N 1992, THE COMMITTEE of Sponsoring Organizations of the Treadway Commission (known as COSO), developed and issued a framework for internal control design. According to its website, www.coso.org, "the Committee is a joint initiative of The American Accounting Association, The American Institute of CPAs, Financial Executives International, The Association of Accountants and Financial Professionals in Business, and The Institute of Internal Auditors. COSO is dedicated to providing thought leadership through the development of frameworks and guidance on enterprise risk management, internal control and fraud deterrence."

The COSO internal control framework is a picture of the proper design of an internal control structure. It contains certain elements that must be included in developing internal controls as a part of an anti-fraud program. There have been certain modifications of the framework recently, but the overall elemental design has stood the test of time for more than 20 years.

 THE ELEMENTS OF ANTI-FRAUD PROGRAM DESIGN

The original COSO framework outlines five elements of internal control design: (1) the control environment, (2) risk assessment, (3) control activities,

1. Anti-Fraud Environment
2. Fraud Risk Assessment
3. Control Activities
4. Information: Program Documentation
5. Communication: The Company Fraud Training Program
6. Monitoring and Routine Maintenance

FIGURE 1.1   Revised Six Elements

(4) information and communication, and (5) monitoring. While keeping with the intent of this structure, I have modified the names and format of some of these elements to best present the architect's blueprint for the design process of the anti-fraud program. The revised six elements are shown in Figure 1.1.

Each reference to program design in this book includes a categorization of the guidance into one or more of these elements. As the elements are addressed, more specific definitions of each will be provided. However, a basic description of each element is provided next to familiarize you with the concepts.

ANTI-FRAUD ENVIRONMENT

The anti-fraud environment is best described as the tone at the top. What is the level of concern for fraud prevention from the business owner, the board of directors, or those bodies tasked with governance of the company? If there is no concern from these parties, assuredly there will be no concern from those below. Conversely, if the owners or governing bodies of a company exhibit an appropriate concern for fraud prevention, then the staff should follow suit.

Evidence of these concerns is demonstrated through the anti-fraud environment: the environment that includes processes and policies established to address fraud risk. Specific best practices for the proper design of a sound anti-fraud environment are presented throughout further sections of this book.

FRAUD RISK ASSESSMENT

In my experience, I have seen that fraud risk assessment is the most neglected of the six elements. I attribute this to the fact that fraud risk is a concept not dwelled on by most small business owners. Small business owners possess an entrepreneurial spirit, the ability to cast a vision, an understanding of their product or service, and the ability to profit from these attributes. Fraud prevention, accounting, and risk assessment are delegated to the accountants. We all have our own set of gifts and talents that, when working together, provide the best operating results for a company.

However, the responsibility for an effective anti-fraud program lies with those with governing authority over the company. Those individuals may certainly seek the advice of the accountant types in designing the anti-fraud program, but the overall responsibility cannot be delegated away from the governing body.

To illustrate, let's look at one example of a risk assessment issue for a company. Assume Company A sells computer parts, such as chips and the numerous electronic insides of a computer. When considering the risk of fraud in a company like this, we would most likely focus on the sales, billing, and collection processes more than the inventory processes. The risk of fraud in the inventory area may be relatively low since electronic components, while costly in nature, are not necessarily susceptible to quick conversion to cash. Some rogue employee swipes a handful of computer chips. What can the employee do with them? Unless he happens to be a participant in a major underground market for these chips, he probably won't profit much in the way of cash. So the risk assessment team will focus less on inventory fraud risk and more on sales, billing, and collection areas.

Conversely, Company B sells the computers that use Company A's chips and electronics. Now, when considering inventory fraud, there is a whole new level of risk. Company B has a warehouse full of laptop computers. These items are relatively small, fit in a backpack, and are easily converted to cash through sales on the street. A rogue employee carries off a couple of laptops in his backpack every day and sells them on the street for $500 each. That's $1,000 per day. Over the span of 20 working days per month, that adds up to $20,000, or $240,000 annually—which, in my opinion, isn't bad beans! Therefore, Company B's fraud risk is in inventory, whereas Company A's lies in another area entirely.

This type of thought process is necessary to understanding how to perform a fraud risk assessment. Because of the importance of this aspect of the framework, an entire chapter is devoted to this subject.

 ## CONTROL ACTIVITIES

This element of internal control is represented by the actual checks and balances that exist. Control activities are *specific*. One of the most common is the bank reconciliation. The performance of the bank reconciliation is a major business process that can also function as an outstanding control activity. If done correctly, bank reconciliations serve not only to prevent fraud but also to detect fraud. Requiring dual signatures on checks over a certain dollar amount and physical inventory counts are excellent examples of specific control activities. Their design is of such importance that I have devoted several chapters to control activities as they apply to various financial areas common in most businesses.

 ## INFORMATION: PROGRAM DOCUMENTATION

In our journey to design the best possible anti-fraud program for your business, we have established a proper anti-fraud environment, assessed the areas of greatest fraud risk, and designed specific control activities to address those risks. Now we need to document that system.

The *information* aspect of this element speaks to the need to commit this program to written form. I consider myself moderately intelligent, but there is no way I would be able to memorize all of the aspects of an anti-fraud program. Committing all of this to written form sounds relatively simple, yet I constantly encounter companies whose anti-fraud strategies are known only by those performing the activities. What happens when these individuals are hit by the proverbial bus? Once they're gone, so is the program, because the replacements won't know it exists. While simple in concept, the process of documentation can become too complex very quickly. This book includes a separate chapter devoted to how to avoid the pitfall of overcomplexity. Remember our motto: *Simple practicality.*

 ## COMMUNICATION: THE COMPANY FRAUD TRAINING PROGRAM

Once the program is in written form, it must be *communicated* to staff, to those who will be responsible for carrying out the program. Do we send out memos? Do we give everyone a binder? Do we have live meetings? Is the program posted on our intranet? Do we periodically conduct training for staff as to how the program works? Do we seek input on problems encountered in carrying out the designed controls? Yes. The answer is a resounding yes. All of these combined represent the best communication efforts. How to combine these efforts to achieve the most effective communication is addressed in further chapters.

Communication is important in both our personal and business relationships. My wife and I have been married for 30 years. Without proper communication, I'm not sure we could have made it this long. Suppose we left our wedding ceremony 30 years ago and never spoke again. That's ludicrous; that's silly to even think about. Yet, more companies than not treat the communication of the anti-fraud program exactly like this. The work is done. Someone said we had to do it. So we did it. We put it in the most beautiful binder imaginable! Then we proudly put it on the shelf and never looked at it again. That's ludicrous; that's silly to even think about.

 ## MONITORING AND ROUTINE MAINTENANCE

The second most neglected element in anti-fraud program design is monitoring and routine maintenance. Monitoring is the built-in process of periodically determining compliance with all aspects of the anti-fraud program. If certain staff members are not complying with the controls in place, we should go the extra step and ask why. Is it a problem with the individual or with the design of the control? Regardless of how this question is answered, there is either someone or something that needs to be fixed.

An anti-fraud program is not a static program. It is a living, breathing document that needs to change based on operational changes. If we don't ever monitor the controls for effectiveness and efficiency, how will we know what needs changing?

Consider in our building metaphor that we have completed the construction of our new home. Obviously, we will move in and live there, possibly forever. Let's assume that through the years we perform no routine maintenance on this home. Eventually it will fall apart and lose all of its effectiveness as a home. Allowing this to happen to your home would be considered extremely irresponsible. The monitoring element of the anti-fraud program is essential to the accomplishment of routine maintenance. Without it, the program will eventually fall apart and lose its effectiveness as a program.

• • •

These six elements provide the framework into which everything we address from this point forward will fit. Think of this framework as the architect's blueprint for a new home. It is the plan for going forward. Without this plan, this blueprint, this framework, our structure will be unsound, ineffective, and possibly even dangerous.

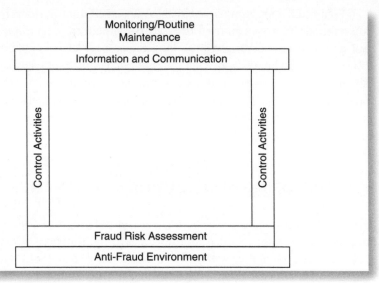

FIGURE 1.2   Framework

The *anti-fraud environment* is the foundation, the *fraud risk assessment* is the ground floor, the *control activities* are the walls (the structure), the *information and communication* elements tie it all together as the ceiling, and the *monitoring and routine maintenance* element tops it off under one roof.

2

Foundational Policies

The Fraud Policy

T WAS A LATE AFTERNOON in the summer of 1998, and I was ready to get home to my family. The courtroom was relatively full because the trial involved a local woman with many friends. I knew I had done a great job of putting the forensic case together and testifying. All that was left were jury deliberations, the rendering of a guilty verdict, and then I could leave with my chest puffed out and my head held high. In retrospect, I should have remembered that pride comes before a fall. Eventually, the jury returned after taking much longer than anticipated in their deliberations. "Oh well," I thought. "I won't get home as early as I thought, but at least I'll have the full weekend to rest." The judge called for the verdict from the jury foreman. "We, the jury, find the defendant not guilty."

"What? How could this be?" I thought, exasperated. It was obvious from the gasps in the courtroom that I wasn't the only one who felt this way. I knew the defendant was guilty of fraud. The gallery knew, the judge knew, the attorneys knew, and, dare I say, even the defendant knew she was guilty. After the courtroom was cleared, I inquired of a juror how they could have possibly reached this verdict. "Mr. Dawson, the company never told her that it was wrong to steal."

FOUNDATIONAL POLICIES

I have come to the conclusion that there are certain absolute policies that every small business must have in place. I have read more policies than I can even remember, a policy for this situation and that situation, even a policy on how to go to the bathroom at work. But as I consider the absolute foundational policies that define and set the proper anti-fraud environment, the proper tone at the top, I have settled on what I call the policies of protection:

- Fraud policy
- Fraud reporting policy
- Expense reimbursement policy

When I refer to the policies of protection, I'm considering protection for not only the assets of the company but also the employees of the company. As the contents of this chapter are discussed, please note that we will use the terms *governing body* and *management* interchangeably. To avoid the risk of another unjust verdict because no one explicitly stated that it is wrong to steal, I begin with what I consider to be the highest absolute.

 ## THE FRAUD POLICY: THE ESSENTIAL ELEMENTS OF AN EFFECTIVE FRAUD POLICY

The fraud policy accomplishes the task of telling an employee that it is wrong to steal. My governing body, the Association of Certified Fraud Examiners (ACFE), has an excellent sample policy for use as a fraud policy. Certain elements presented here have been influenced by that policy, and certain elements have been added based on my experiences. The policy does not have to be a certain length to be considered a good policy; rather, it has to include 11 basic elements that influence its overall effectiveness.

Element 1. Policy Statement

- Establishes that management is responsible for the prevention and detection of fraud.
- Encourages management to be familiar with the types of fraud that can occur.

Comments: This is not a responsibility that can be delegated to outside parties. I have performed services for a number of companies whose management does not understand this concept. I performed the annual financial statement audit for one company whose management made this statement to me every year for three consecutive years, "We don't need internal controls. Fraud is never going to happen here. We have good people." When I hear this statement, I immediately form an opinion that the anti-fraud environment is nonexistent. This kind of statement is indicative of complete denial or of management that is in the midst of perpetrating fraud. It would make a good example if I could say that this manager and his company ultimately experienced a fraud occurrence. It would make an even better example if I could show you that this manager and his company ultimately experienced numerous frauds. Unfortunately, this is exactly what happened. Although certainly not seeking vindication, I have to admit that there was some satisfaction in thinking, "I told you so."

Sample Policy Statement

The management of MED Enterprises is responsible for the prevention and detection of fraud. All parties should be familiar with the types of fraud that might occur and should be alert for any indication of fraud.

Element 2. Scope

▪ Establishes the parties subject to this policy.

Comments: A common mistake is to consider that the only parties subject to this fraud policy are employees. It should be understood that the policy applies to everyone: employees, board members, vendors, and any others doing business with the company.

Sample Scope

This policy applies equally to any fraudulent activity involving not only employees but also directors, vendors, outside agencies, and/or unknown parties without regard to length of service, title or position, or relationship.

Element 3. Actions Constituting Fraud

▪ Provides an indication of what is considered to be fraud.
▪ Is purposefully *general* in nature.
▪ Leaves the door open for "what might be considered fraud."

Comments: It is impossible to place every potential type or nature of fraud into a single policy. This policy section is designed to provide general example areas that any of a thousand different instances of fraud may fit. Remember, one of the primary objectives of the fraud policy is to prove that the company has made the statement that it is wrong to steal.

Sample Actions Constituting Fraud

The terms *fraud*, *misappropriation*, and *irregularities* refer, but are not limited, to:

- Any dishonest act
- Misapplication of funds or assets
- Profiting on insider knowledge
- Destruction of records or assets
- Disclosure of confidential information
- Forgery or alteration of documents
- Impropriety in reporting transactions
- Gifts from vendors (outside of limits)
- Disappearance of records or assets
- Any similar or related irregularity

Element 4. Nonfraud Irregularities

- Establishes that moral or behavioral issues, when disruptive to the workforce, should be investigated by departments other than audit departments or audit-related organizations.

    Comments: Moral and behavioral issues run the spectrum from talking too loudly on the phone, to torrid office love affairs, to drug abuse in the workplace. These disruptive issues should be dealt with swiftly and severely, more appropriately by management or human resources personnel and not by audit department personnel.

Sample Nonfraud Irregularities

Identification or allegations of personal improprieties or irregularities, whether moral or behavioral, should be resolved by departmental management, executive management, and/or the human resources department, rather than by audit-related departments or agencies.

Element 5. Reporting Structure

- References the process in place for an employee to report suspicions of fraud.

- Provides assurance that whistle-blower protection provisions are in place for reporting under the referenced structure.
- Provides the warning that under no circumstances should an individual attempt to confront the accused or conduct his or her own investigation.

Comments: The provisions in this element direct you to the separate policy that outlines the process for reporting suspicions of fraud. The various formats available for a fraud reporting policy are addressed in the next chapter. Depending on the organization, a whistle-blower protection provision can be included in the fraud policy or in a separate policy altogether. This element of the policy references that there is a protection provision, whether in this policy or in a separate policy. I have witnessed the legal disasters that can occur when employees take it upon themselves to confront the suspect or perform their own investigation. This element strictly prohibits this type of handling of fraud suspicions.

Sample Reporting Structure

The {board of directors or owners} of the organization have established a formal reporting mechanism whereby any individual who has knowledge of any suspected fraudulent activity can anonymously report these suspicions. Please reference the MED Enterprises "Fraud Reporting Policy" for the proper reporting of suspicions. Any individual making a notification in accordance with the "Fraud Reporting Policy" is protected by the whistle-blower protection provisions of this fraud policy. In no circumstance should an individual confront the fraud suspect or attempt an investigation.

Element 6. Investigation Responsibilities

- Establishes that, with proper predication, the responsible investigation parties (audit committee, owner, etc.) *must* perform or cause to be performed an investigation into the allegations.
- Establishes that any investigation performed must be properly documented.
- Establishes that prosecution decisions will be made in conjunction with legal counsel.

Comments: Predication is more commonly referred to as "reasonable cause." Therefore, with enough proof of reasonable cause, a properly conducted and documented investigation is required. Additional information regarding what does and does not constitute reasonable cause is provided in Chapter 3.

This element also requires the inclusion of legal counsel in the decision-making process regarding prosecution or ultimate disposition of the case.

One of the most effective fraud deterrents is the knowledge that suspicions of fraud will be investigated. I have seen time and again the frustration experienced by employees when they believe that management is ignoring or sweeping under the carpet suspicions of fraud. The overall effectiveness of the fraud policy and the anti-fraud program is significantly enhanced when employees know that their concerns will be addressed.

Sample Investigation Responsibilities

Upon receipt of notification of alleged fraudulent activities, the {responsible parties as defined in the Fraud Reporting Policy} must investigate the specific allegations utilizing available internal and/or external resources. The {responsible parties} shall retain in its possession all documentation regarding the nature of the allegations, the date the allegations were received, the resolution of the allegations, and the date resolved. Decisions to refer investigation results to the appropriate authorities for prosecution will be made in conjunction with legal counsel, the board of directors, and senior management.

Element 7. Authorization for Investigation

■ Establishes that the parties responsible for the investigation have full access to the premises, company records, and office location of the suspect, including personal property of the suspect on company premises.

Comments: Without access to all of the records and premises of the organization, an investigator cannot possibly obtain the proper evidence necessary to present in court. This section implicitly speaks to the issue of the presumption of privacy, which should be explicitly stated in other organizational policies, such as the employee manual or personnel policies. Do the employees of the organization presume that their workspace, along with all items in it, is their private area? If so, there will be significant investigation and ensuing legal difficulties. Personnel policies or employee manuals should be clear in removing this presumption of privacy. Regardless of how this may be viewed, it is critically important that employees understand this is your company and your property and that they work for you. They should understand that nothing on company premises is theirs and that investigators may have access to all files, personal items, e-mail, and so forth left on company premises.

Sample Authorization for Investigation

Those individuals or agencies assigned the responsibility for investigation may take control of and gain full access to the organization's records and premises without prior consent of any individual who may have custody of any such records or premises.

Element 8. Acting in Good Faith

- Addresses the courses of action to be taken against an individual who makes false or malicious allegations.

Comments: This element is critically important in protecting the organization against obviously false or maliciously reported allegations. As discussed in Chapter 3, employees often have an axe to grind against other employees. Without policy provisions to safeguard the organization and to control these types of reported allegations, the audit department or responsible investigative parties could be overrun with frivolous investigations that ultimately weaken the anti-fraud program.

Sample Acting in Good Faith

Any individual reporting any irregularity in accordance with the fraud reporting policy must be acting in good faith and have reasonable grounds for believing the information provided. Allegations made maliciously or with knowledge of their falsity will not be tolerated. Individuals making such allegations may be subject to organizational disciplinary action and/or legal actions by the individuals accused of fraudulent conduct.

Element 9. Whistle-Blower Protection

- Establishes protection for retaliation against those who have reported suspicions of fraud in accordance with the fraud reporting policy.
- Outlines how to report issues of retaliation.
- Dictates that management may still "manage" employees in the normal course of their assigned functions.

Comments: Whistle-blower protection law is complex. Management should seek legal counsel in understanding all of the various definitions of *retaliation*. It is imperative that whistle-blower protection provisions be included in the fraud policy, a separate whistle-blower protection policy, or the fraud reporting policy. For purposes of this sample policy, these provisions have been included as part of the fraud policy.

This element also addresses the situation where management, for fear of being accused of retaliation, feels powerless to correct, discipline, or even terminate a whistle-blower for non-whistle-blower-related issues, such as job performance. I have witnessed firsthand the detrimental effects on an organization when management has this fear. An organization is only as strong as the weakest link, and carrying that weak link beyond the appropriate time results in low employee morale and low productivity.

Sample Whistle-Blower Protection

Employees may not retaliate against a whistle-blower for reporting an activity that person believes to be fraudulent or dishonest. Retaliation can be evidenced by the intent of adversely affecting the terms or conditions of employment (including, but not limited to, threats of physical harm, dismissal, transfer to an undesirable job assignment, demotion, suspension, or impact on salary or wages). The whistle-blower is defined as an employee who reports allegations of fraud in accordance with the provisions of the fraud reporting policy. Whistle-blowers who believe that they have been retaliated against may file a written complaint with {responsible party such as corporate legal counsel}. Any complaint of retaliation will be promptly investigated by the {responsible party}, and appropriate measures will be taken if allegations of retaliation are proven. This protection from retaliation is not intended to prohibit managers or supervisors from taking action, including disciplinary action, in the usual scope of their duties and based on valid performance-related factors.

Element 10. Suspension or Termination

- Establishes what will happen to the suspected employee during the performance of and after the investigation.
- Establishes that all fraud will be prosecuted to the fullest extent of the law.

Comments: Generally, placing the accused on administrative leave with pay is the most common treatment of the employee during the investigation. However, I have performed numerous covert investigations where the suspect employees are still serving in their assigned function. The nature of the allegations tends to determine when an employee should be placed on leave. Common sense and sound legal advice should be considered when making the determination of placing a suspect employee on administrative leave, reinstatement, and/or termination. Any and all issues associated with the treatment of the suspect employee must occur in the presence of and at the advice of the organization's legal counsel.

Sample Suspension or Termination

During an investigation, the suspected individual may be suspended with pay. Based on the results of the investigation, the individual will be either reinstated or terminated under the direction of organizational legal counsel. Fraudulent activities will be prosecuted to the fullest extent of the law.

Element 11. Acknowledgment and Signature

- Provides written proof that the organization told employees that it is wrong to steal, including acknowledgment by the employees that they understand fraud will not be tolerated.

Comments: It is difficult to state that one element of the fraud policy is more important than another, but when considering the implications of this element, the case could be made that this is the most important paragraph in the policy.

One of the first questions I ask management as part of an investigation is, "Do you have a fraud policy?" Because we must apparently tell employees it is wrong to steal, I feel this to be one of the most important questions in establishing a case.

 CASE PRESENTATION

I asked this question of the manager of an organization as part of an investigation, and he told me, "No, we don't have any policy like that." Right away, I knew how this could end, but I continued my investigative work regardless. As I was looking through a filing cabinet, I noticed a manila folder with "fraud policy" written on the tab. I looked in the folder and found an outstanding fraud policy, one page in length but inclusive of all necessary provisions for a company of its size. I also noticed that there was a fraud policy that had been signed by each employee in the organization, including the suspect employee.

I took this information back to the manager and said, "I thought you didn't have a fraud policy." He looked over the papers I brought to him and responded, "Oh yeah, I remember this now. Yeah, this is the fraud policy that we give to each employee during their orientation. You know, when we give them all of the papers like the medical insurance enrollment forms, the 401(k) forms, we give them this policy to sign as well. Yes, Steve, I was wrong, we do have a fraud policy." My only response was "No, you don't."

If your employees have no recollection of signing a fraud policy, or if your employees are not constantly reminded of the existence of the fraud policy, then you have no fraud policy. You may have one in form, but certainly not in substance. A workforce that doesn't remember the existence of the policy is a workforce that works within a poor anti-fraud environment.

It is imperative that the fraud policy and the fraud reporting policy should be reviewed with staff no less frequently than annually (see Figure 2.1). This should be a part of the periodic fraud awareness training that is discussed later in this book. The annual review and re-signing of this policy is an absolute must. Anything less will render the policy completely ineffective.

I cannot state strongly enough that your organization *must* have a fraud policy inclusive of the provisions outlined in this chapter. I see often that some organizations have a separate ethics policy or refer to their fraud policy as an ethics policy or even a code of conduct. That's fine, but however you refer to it, the policy has to include these necessary provisions.

As a public speaker, I am often asked, "What happens when an investigation results in the fact that a false accusation was made?" The answer to that question is that it depends. If your organization has a fraud policy such as presented in this chapter, you are well protected. If not, well, it can get really ugly, really quickly. The liability to the organization is unlimited. The fraud policy is a *policy of protection*. Don't conduct business another day without it.

I have read and understand the contents of this fraud policy. I understand that the organization will not tolerate fraudulent or dishonest activities of any kind and that I am not to engage in such acts while employed by MED Enterprises.

_____

Signature

_____

Date

FIGURE 2.1   Sample Acknowledgment and Signature

CHAPTER THREE

Foundational Policies

The Fraud Reporting Policy

I N THE MIDST OF BEING A certified fraud examiner, I was also a financial statement auditor for 26 years. As a result, I often had the opportunity to know the employees of an organization, and they knew me as well. As I reflect on my career thus far, one of these unique relationships stands out in my mind mainly because it scared me so badly.

I was working late, alone in my first-floor downtown office. My office had full-length vertical windows. Anyone passing by could see in with no problem; however, it was impossible for me to see outside in the darkness. I was already somewhat anxious being alone at such a late hour when I heard a loud knock . . . at my window! To say that I jumped out of my skin is an understatement. Unable to see out of my window, I ran to the front entrance of our building to find a 60-year-old woman waiting for me to let her in. It was Phyllis, an employee of one of my audit clients. She was desperate and visibly distraught. She was there to tell me that the manager of her organization was involved in committing fraud and had been for seven years. As we sat and talked, she provided information on how the fraud worked and how the manager had concealed it from us, the auditors, for such a long time. She told me that she could no longer sleep, could not enjoy her job, and even considered suicide to get away from it all. The more she talked, the calmer she became. She told me, "There just hasn't been any way that I could tell the board of directors or an audit committee because we don't have any program in place to report these kinds of things. I feel like I am alone on an island, and I want off!"

The proper anti-fraud environment has to include a mechanism, a process, by which employees can feel comfortable in reporting suspicions of fraud. Every two years, the Association of Certified Fraud Examiners issues the *Report to the Nations on Occupational Fraud and Abuse.* The ACFE gathers information from us, its fraud examiners, to compile this information into an outstanding statistical look at what is going on in the fraud world. One of the statistics that has remained consistent since the inception of the report is that tips are the number one way that fraud is detected.

When fraud is occurring in an organization, someone else probably knows it's happening or at least suspects that it's happening. Without the ability to tell someone, that employee's anxiety can increase exponentially, even to the point of considering suicide. My story here is not an isolated case. I have relived that same anxious, distraught, potential whistle-blower scenario multiple times.

A proper fraud reporting policy provides employees with the opportunity to tell their story. A simple procedure provides a way off that hopeless island and ensures security for those with crucial information who desire to come forward.

THE ESSENTIAL ELEMENTS OF AN EFFECTIVE FRAUD REPORTING POLICY

A properly designed, properly functioning fraud reporting mechanism results in a significant positive effect on the anti-fraud environment. This fraud reporting mechanism can be, and often is, included in the fraud policy. To provide clarity, I have presented it in this chapter as a separate policy. The essential elements, descriptive bullet points, my comments, and sample policy provisions are as follows.

Element 1. Policy Statement

- Establishes that management takes the issue of fraud seriously and understands the importance of providing a fraud reporting mechanism.

Comments: To exhibit a proper anti-fraud environment and to communicate to the workforce that you as management care about the importance of fraud prevention, a fraud reporting mechanism is absolutely necessary. The proper functioning of this policy eliminates the need for your employees to knock on someone's window in the middle of the night. It alleviates the anxiety and the pain of wanting to do the right thing but not knowing how to go about it. And as we consider the policies of protection, we see that this protects not only the organization but also the employee.

Sample Policy Statement

As referenced in the fraud policy of MED Enterprises, {responsible parties} has established this policy to provide a framework for reporting suspicions of fraud. MED Enterprises commits to properly addressing the concerns of employees as submitted in accordance with the provisions of this policy.

Element 2. Scope

- Establishes the parties subject to this policy.

   Comments: This element makes clear that the ability to report suspicions of fraud is not confined to just employees. Board members, vendors, and others doing business with the organization can report suspicions of fraud as well.

Sample Scope

It is understood that employees, directors, vendors, and other outside agencies may make a report of suspicions of fraud under this policy. It is also understood that the scope of this policy can include reporting suspicions of fraudulent activity allegedly performed by employees, directors, vendors, or other outside agencies, against the organization.

Element 3. Reportable Actions Constituting Fraud

- Provides an indication of what is considered to be a reportable fraudulent activity.
- As with the fraud policy, is purposefully *general* in nature.

   Comments: Typically, the workforce in general does not understand what fraud is. My experience has shown that if you ask 10 people about suspicions of fraud within their organization, you will get eight different answers. Some believe I am asking about external fraud against their organization; others focus on what could be called unethical acts but not fraud. Others simply respond with "What's that?"

As compared with the fraud policy, this policy includes a brief educational synopsis of what we are really asking for when we ask for tips about fraudulent activity. The three types of fraud are as follows:

1. **Asset misappropriation:** Simply stated, this is taking company assets for personal gain. Historically, this is the most common type of occupational or internal fraud committed against an organization. The various subcategories of asset misappropriation are beyond the scope of a fraud reporting policy but should be included as part of periodic fraud awareness training, as discussed in Chapter 11.
2. **Corruption:** This type of fraud is collusion between two or more employees or an employee and an outside party, such as a vendor. This type of fraud includes, but is not limited to, the subcategories of bribery, illegal gratuities, kickback schemes, and bid rigging in contract procurement.
3. **Financial statement fraud:** This is the intentional manipulation of reported financial results: "Let's make this number better so we will meet our debt covenant ratio requirements" or "Let's make this number worse so we can save on income taxes." These are just two examples of why people commit financial statement fraud.

Although the policy does not go into this level of detail, it does provide enough information to give the reporting party some confidence in what he or she is reporting. Of course, this information is strengthened when considered in conjunction with periodic fraud awareness training, discussed in Chapter 11.

Sample Reportable Actions Constituting Fraud

Fraud, *misappropriation*, and *irregularities* are synonymous terms commonly used to refer to occupational or internal fraud. There are three types of fraud: asset misappropriation (the taking of company assets), corruption (collusion between at least two parties to gain personally while causing a loss to the company), and financial statement fraud (misrepresenting the financial position and/or results of operations). Fraud can include, but is not limited to, any dishonest act, misapplication of funds or assets, profiting on insider knowledge, destruction of records or assets, disclosure of confidential information, forgery or alteration of documents, impropriety in reporting transactions, gifts from vendors (outside of limits), disappearance of records or assets, and/or any similar or related irregularity.

Element 4. Predication

- Defines for the reader certain criteria of predication, or reasonable cause, that should be considered when making a report under this policy.
- Reinforces that knowingly making a false or frivolous report is prohibited by this policy.

Comments: I have received countless tips from employees accusing other employees of committing fraud. Statistically, about 30 percent of these tips are worthy of an investigation. Why is this number so low? I submit that it is primarily because many employees have what I call axes to grind against one another. So how do I determine whether a tip is valid? The answer lies in the concept of predication.

What is predication? It is the white-collar crime equivalent of the street crime term for reasonable cause. A police officer cannot simply decide to search your home without your permission. If the officer has suspicions of what he may find in your home, he obtains a search warrant from a judge to perform the search legally. To obtain the search warrant, he must tell the judge what he anticipates finding in your home that would provide evidence to support his suspicions of your illegal activities. In other words, he must prove that there is reasonable cause to search your premises.

We as fraud examiners must have an idea that something illegal may have occurred in the records of the organization. Relying on someone's word alone is not enough to commence an investigation. There has to be some type of evidence, not proof, but evidence sufficient to conclude that there is indeed a legitimate concern. This is predication. "You say something is happening in your organization, but why do you say that? What can you show me that caused you to make this report under this policy?"

I have received the most troubling answers when I ask this question. "Well, Jim's just a crook, everyone knows it," or "I saw her steal from the teacher's desk when we had the same class in the eighth grade," or even "he's having an affair with my wife and I want him out of here."

You can see that the determination of significant predication is a difficult task. Accordingly, this policy attempts to head off at the pass these personal or paranoid issues before launching a potentially frivolous investigation.

It should be emphasized that the type of information that supports predication is not necessarily proof evidence. To make a report under this policy, proof is not needed. In no circumstance should potential reporters feel that they need verifiable proof before something will be investigated. There just needs to be some information that supports the need to look further into the matter. As an example, consider the following scenario:

In reviewing payments on the company credit card, the accounting clerk notices that the full balance is not being paid each month by the company. However, when the following month's statement is received, the balance is zero, and there are two payments reflected on the statement. Something just doesn't look right. After a report is made under the fraud reporting policy, it is determined that with several monthly credit card statements in hand, an investigation into the matter is proper. The investigation does reveal that something isn't right. It seems the accounting supervisor uses the company credit card for personal purposes every month. At the end of each month, she adds up her personal use and pays the credit card directly with a personal check. She then pays the business use portion with a company check. As a result, there is no loss to the company, no personal benefit to her, and thus no fraud. However, this type of accounting should not occur and should cease immediately.

My own investigation practice reflects that approximately 52 percent of the investigations I perform result in the conclusion that fraud has not occurred. It may show an error in the recording of transactions or an error in judgment, but not an occurrence of fraud. There was enough predication to support an investigation because there was a significant problem that needed to be addressed, but it just wasn't fraud.

Therefore, potential reporters should not feel that they cannot make a report without verifiable proof of the fraud. After all, that is the investigator's job and area of expertise.

Sample Predication, or Reasonable Cause

The company has implemented this policy to encourage the reporting of suspicions that fraud is occurring or has been perpetrated against the organization. It is understood that in making a report in accordance with this policy, proof positive evidence is not necessary. The potential reporter does not have to be right. The potential reporter should simply consider what predication, or reasonable cause, exists to make a report. Accordingly, those considering making a report under this policy should provide some type of documentation that a fraud may have been committed or at least indicate that the specific issue may appear to be fraudulent in nature. It is the responsibility of the investigators to form the conclusion that presentable fraud has occurred. Maliciously false or frivolous reports made under this policy will be dealt with in accordance with the provisions noted in the fraud policy.

Element 5. Reporting Mechanism

■ Provides details of how suspicions may be reported.

Comments: This element represents the core of the policy. It is this section of the policy that can vary widely between different organizations. The objective of this section is to provide clear and simple instructions on how a potential reporter may submit or make a report to the responsible party. One of the key factors that must be addressed is the decision about providing anonymity for the reporter.

Regardless of the size of the organization, I believe each and every organization should provide an anonymous reporting mechanism. Outside of that requirement, the programs may differ significantly.

Step 1. Determine Who Receives the Fraud Notification

Who should receive the notifications? Typically, the highest level of the organization, the governing body, represents the recipient of the fraud notification. The governing body can be a board of directors, an audit committee, a separate committee of the board of directors, or the owner(s) of the business {the responsible party}. In some circumstances, the organization chooses to have its in-house legal counsel receive the notifications, or, in the absence of in-house counsel, the organization chooses to use its retained external legal counsel.

Step 2. Determine How the Notification Is to Be Received

Written notification: A simple form should be developed that seeks as much information as possible. The major drawback to an anonymous reporting mechanism is that you get only one chance to obtain information. You will not be able to ask the reporting party further questions unless he or she voluntarily provides a name. The administration of the notification aspect of the program is relatively simple in that the form submission should be mailed to a designated address or placed in a designated locked box for access by the responsible party. The form can also be e-mailed to a designated e-mail address by a disguised sender e-mail, but most people do not have the sophistication—or time, for that matter—to use this method (see Figure 3.1).

To ensure effectiveness of the fraud reporting mechanism, the form should be made available to everyone through the employee manual or posted on the company intranet for easy access by the potential reporter. I have seen well-designed programs lose their effectiveness with the statement: "Form FN-1 may

---

	Form FN-1

ANONYMOUS SUBMISSION OF ALLEGATIONS OF FRAUD

Date Submitted: _____   ***Do NOT provide your name***

Submitted by: (Optional)

☐ Employee
☐ Customer/Member
☐ Vendor
☐ Other _____

Specific Allegation(s):

Please provide a description of the alleged fraudulent activity, including the suspected individual's(s') name(s) and position within the organization. Please attach any supporting documentation you might have regarding the alleged violation.

_____
_____
_____
_____
_____
_____
_____
_____
_____
_____
_____

FIGURE 3.1   Form FN-1: Anonymous Submission of Allegations of Fraud

be obtained from the director of human resources." Well, what happened to anonymity? A potential reporter who wants to remain anonymous is certainly not going to drop in to the human resources department to ask for a form. This is just a simple illustration that every aspect of the program needs to be run through a commonsense filter.

Telephone notification: As an alternative to the written notification, the organization may provide the telephone number of a fraud hotline to call to report suspicions of fraud. Before undertaking the herculean task of managing your own internal fraud hotline, you should consider utilizing a company that provides this service. All administration of the hotline is handled by the company with professional staff trained to obtain information when there may only be a single opportunity to obtain the information. The price of this service is certainly worth not having to maintain and manage an internal hotline.

If you choose to manage your own fraud hotline, the points to consider are substantial. Various aspects that must be considered and determined are as follows:

- Operating hours
- Interview training for hotline workers
- Determine if other issues will be handled by the hotline (moral or behavioral issues)
- How information obtained is to be distributed
- Determine escalation criteria (threats, threat levels, immediate business interruption, etc.) and the training necessary to properly assess escalation issues
- Print the hotline number on checks, invoices, letterhead

As can be seen, the internal administration of a fraud hotline is costly and difficult to staff for most small businesses. Additionally, the risk of creating liability for the company from improper training could be substantial. For most small businesses, contracting with an external hotline provider may be the most effective and efficient method of providing an anonymous reporting mechanism.

Sample Reporting Mechanism

The {board of directors}, {owners} of the organization have established a formal reporting mechanism whereby any individual who has knowledge of any suspected fraudulent activity can anonymously report these suspicions. The reporting process is as follows: {the remainder of this section provides the details of the selected processes provided in steps 1 and 2 in the comments}. Notifications made in accordance with this policy will be handled according to the provisions of the separate fraud policy of MED Enterprises.

Element 6. Acknowledgment and Signature

■ Provides for written acknowledgment by the employee that he or she understands that an anonymous reporting mechanism is in place for reporting suspicions of fraud.

Comments: One of the most disheartening experiences in my profession is to see the face of, or hear the voice of, an individual who has lived with the pressure of not being able to make a fraud notification report when he or she truly believes something should be investigated. Obtaining the acknowledgment of the employee provides evidence that the organization has communicated the existence of this policy to the workforce.

Sample Acknowledgment and Signature

I have read and understand the contents of this fraud reporting policy.

_____

Signature

_____

Date

Considering the necessary tone-at-the-top aspect of a sound anti-fraud environment, this existence of an anonymous fraud reporting mechanism tells the employee that management cares. It tells them that management cares about the organization, the employees, and the prevention and detection of fraud. In concert with the fraud policy, the two policies, the *policies of protection*, provide the very foundation of a properly designed anti-fraud environment.

4

Foundational Policies

The Expense Reimbursement Policy

THE FRAUD AND FRAUD REPORTING policies represent general policies of protection that serve as the foundation of a strong anti-fraud environment. There are numerous other policies to be considered that specifically address certain issues including Internet usage, e-mail usage, and personal use of computers; however, these policies can be considered more of a control activity.

I now firmly believe a specific policy needs to be raised to the level of a foundational policy. Credit and debit card usage, which also includes the normal provisions of the expense and travel reimbursement policy, has become a policy of absolute necessity. As a unit, this will be described as the expense reimbursement policy.

 ## CASE: "NO QUESTIONS ASKED"

Ann was responsible for reserving meeting rooms for corporate training events for her company. There were weeks when she had three or four of these events to schedule. After about six months of working for the company, Ann devised a way to substantially supplement her modest salary. She would call a hotel or convention center and ask for a faxed quote for the cost of reserving a meeting room for 200 participants. The quote amounted to approximately $8,000. She would then submit this faxed quote to her company for reimbursement, stating that she paid for the event with her personal credit card. With no questions asked, her company would reimburse her for the full amount. The actual event was intended to include only about 100 participants. When the event occurred, the actual cost was $4,500, which Ann paid for with her personal credit card. As such, Ann was able to profit $3,500 from this one training event. With this kind of profit, it didn't take long for Ann's ill-gotten gains to accumulate to a substantial amount.

 ## CASE: "IT WILL NEVER BE MISSED"

A company employee devised a way to profit one dollar every day. She paid for a business lunch every day with her personal credit card. On the merchant copy of the credit card receipt, she would tip her server five dollars. She would then take the customer copy of the receipt, write in a six-dollar tip, and submit it to her employer for reimbursement. In doing so, she profited one dollar from the fraudulent expense reimbursement. The fraud was detected when she got careless and submitted a receipt with a four-dollar tip written on the receipt for the purchase of a book.

The fascinating issue with these two cases is that the person in the second case is the same person as in the first case. Why would Ann get so greedy? She was able to perform fraudulent transactions that amounted to more than $10,000 every week, yet still had to get that extra dollar from the business lunch fraud. When asked why, she said, "Because it was easy; why not?"

I have lost count of how many investigations I have performed that involved charging personal items to the company credit card or by using the debit card. I have lost count of the investigations I have performed that involved fictitious travel or other expense reimbursements. I have found this type of fraud so frequently that I now voluntarily look into credit card, travel, and expense reimbursement practices in addition to the specific issue I am asked to investigate. Clients are somewhat surprised each time I present them with the additional fraud they weren't even suspecting. This type of fraud has become so commonplace that I am beginning to believe that every organization is experiencing this fraud; they just don't know it yet.

Accordingly, this chapter is devoted to presenting the necessary elements of what I will refer to as the expense reimbursement policy. The policy addresses and provides coverage for the use of the credit or debit card and provides coverage for reimbursement of travel and other valid business expenses.

 ## CASE: LARRY THE CHIEF FINANCIAL OFFICER

I introduced Larry on the very first page of this book's preface. Larry's story is truly something special. My investigation of his expense reimbursement fraud showed a $1.3 million loss to his company. You would think this would require a lot of maneuvering to accomplish. But what makes Larry's case so special is the ease involved in his perpetration of this fraud. Larry's case serves as the basis for so many different control activities to consider that it is worthy of full presentation here.

As a long-term trusted employee, Larry had served as the chief financial officer for his company for a little over 10 years. Because of significant financial pressures, most caused by family health issues, he felt there was nowhere he could turn for help and thus rationalized that he would borrow company funds for a little while and then pay it back once he weathered these financial crises. Because of the amount of trust that he had earned over the years, his position gave him the opportunity to commit the fraud with ease.

His fraud of choice was simple expense reimbursement fraud. With responsibility for oversight of 13 locations nationwide, Larry had to travel frequently. So with the company credit card in hand, he traversed the country to fulfill his responsibilities. Upon his return to the office after each trip, he would complete the required expense report requesting reimbursement for business use of his personal credit cards (VISA and MasterCard). Most of the time, he would complete the purchase requisition request with the payments to be made directly to his personal credit card companies. But wait, I have already stated that he carried the company credit card with him, the only credit card his company used, the American Express card. So why did his company make payments to VISA and MasterCard with no questions asked?

Company policy also required that all receipts and supporting documentation be attached to the expense report. Larry complied, or at least his employer thought he did. In reality, he would accumulate receipts, mountains of receipts actually, and staple them between two sheets of 8½-by-11 copy paper. When I say "staple," I mean staple. Larry stapled all along the four borders of the copy paper and sometimes in the middle of the sheets. The number of staples used to bind these two pieces of paper should have been considered abusive, at the very least. I remember pulling the staples from one set of documentation that took me 41 minutes to open. What was he hiding so intently?

Once inside these two pieces of paper, I found receipts for just about everything and anything, except any valid cost to the company. I found gas pump receipts that had been left hanging at the pump by the previous customer. Larry scoured gas pumps to find these receipts that had been left behind, just so he could include them as support for expense reimbursement. I found hotel bills for travel stays that occurred from one to five years ago. I found copies of receipts that applied to reimbursements that had been claimed several years in the past. I even found receipts for items that had been paid for with cash (remember the reimbursements were going to credit card companies). I could go on about the different types of receipts I found, none of which related to any type of valid charge for the company. The most egregious example I found were receipts for charges that were paid for with the company American Express card. So not only did the company pay its own American Express bill but also it paid Larry's credit card companies for charges to its own American Express card.

Why was this so easy? There are many reasons. Larry intimidated staff to post journal entries to even out the charges so that the volume of charges didn't accumulate in just one account. Larry never took a vacation for fear that his deeds would be discovered. Larry's tenure and position afforded him the trust of his peers. Finally, the individual responsible for signing the checks never unstapled the documentation sets attached to the expense report for review and validation. The perfect storm, so to speak, and $1.3 million later, Larry is in prison serving out a term that may extend to the end of his life. It is sad and tragic and, quite frankly, unnecessary.

The most tragic aspect of Ann's and Larry's stories is that these are not isolated occurrences. They repeat almost daily in my fraud investigation practice. Because of repeat occurrences such as this, I have elevated the expense reimbursement policy to the foundational level. Let's look at the simplicity of the policy through an examination of the necessary elements:

THE ELEMENTS OF AN EFFECTIVE EXPENSE REIMBURSEMENT POLICY

Element 1. Policy Statement

- Establishes that credit and debit cards will be provided for official company use only.

Comments: The cards should never be used in a system where employees are allowed to charge personal items to the card with the understanding that they will then reimburse the company. For some reason, these personal charges never quite get completely reimbursed to the company.

Sample Policy Statement

It is the intent of MED Enterprises to provide company-issued credit cards and/or bank account–related debit cards for official company use only.

Element 2. Scope

▪ Establishes the parties subject to this policy.

Comments: Any individual who will have a need to use the cards or travel for company business should be identified in this section.

Sample Scope

This policy applies to any and all employed staff, owners, and members of the governing body and to any and all use of the company-issued credit or debit cards and/or cash advances issued for company-related travel.

Element 3. Authorized Uses

▪ Outlines the specific allowable (authorized) uses of the cards.
▪ Specifically includes travel costs.
▪ Specifically includes other business expenses.

Comments: This section is very specific. Unlike generalized policies, the specifics in this section leave no question as to what is considered a permitted use of the cards.

Sample Authorized Uses

Authorized uses of the company-issued cards are as follows:

Travel Costs
Airfare
Lodging
Shuttle service
Rental vehicles

Gasoline for rental vehicles

Meals—documented as outlined in this policy

Purchases

Office supplies

Other expenses when the purchase order process is not available

Element 4. Unauthorized Uses

∎ Establishes very clearly what is not allowed.

Comments: Many policies include provisions that address the same issue in a different manner. As an example, many reimbursement policies allow employees to use their personal credit cards for business use and then have their company reimburse them. This policy example does not allow this scenario and expressly disallows any personal use of the company cards. I hold firm to this position because of Larry and many others just like him. I grow weary of investigating the myriad of issues that arise when personal use and personal charges are allowed in any manner. Accordingly, the policy may seem overly restrictive, but I believe this to be absolutely necessary.

Sample Unauthorized Uses

Unauthorized uses include any personal charge whatsoever, including but not limited to personal meals, personal telephone usage, in-room movies, or in-room minibar usage included on hotel room bills.

Additionally, under no circumstance will the company reimburse the employee for business expenses that were paid for personally by the employee.

Element 5. Violations

∎ Establishes the consequences of violations of the provisions of the policy.

Comments: A policy without consequences is no policy at all. This section dictates that cancellation of the usage privileges for a period of six months and a formal reprimand will be the consequence of the first violation. A subsequent violation will result in termination. The consequences go one step further in stating that an unsupported charge will result in the charge being classified as personal and thus subject to reimbursement by the employee to the company. Again, while many will disagree with the hard stance taken in this policy, I believe it to be absolutely necessary for the protection of company assets.

Sample Violations

The initial violation of the provisions of this policy will result in the removal of the privilege of use for a period of six months and a formal reprimand. Violations related to failure to provide supporting documentation will result in the charge being considered personal and thus subject to refund to the company. A second violation will result in termination.

Element 6. Documentation

▪ Establishes the exact documentation and accounting processes required for compliance with the usage of company cards.
▪ Reinforces the stance that failure to provide the required documentation will result in the charge being considered personal and thus subject to reimbursement by the employee to the company.

Comments: The actual receipt for every charge to the company card or the cash use of a travel advance must be attached as supporting documentation. I continue to see the actual credit card statement being used as the supporting documentation. The actual credit card statement is of very little to no use in establishing the validity of the charge. The statement basically provides the date and location of the charge. The same holds true for monthly credit account statements such as an Office Depot statement. The underlying receipt provides the necessary information on what this purchase is and what it is for. Additionally, because of the ease I have seen in the ability to commit meal and entertainment costs reimbursement fraud, there is a separate section and form that must be completed specific to these types of charges.

Case: "Everyone Needs Office Supplies"

Please understand that I'm not singling out Office Depot. Any large office supply company (Staples, OfficeMax) can be substituted as the name. So I ask whether you have been to an Office Depot lately. I am firmly convinced that everything necessary to sustain human life can be found at an Office Depot.

As you walk in the store, immediately to your left are the checkout counters with chocolate candy and popcorn prominently on display (food). The office supply retailers also supply your company break room, so you will find paper goods such as plates, cups, and utensils (the necessary items to eat your food). Walk down the next aisle, and you will find the bottled water. So now you have food, water, and the necessary paper goods and utensils. There is one more necessary item: toilet paper. The office supplier provides all items to stock the restrooms at your office. So there you have it; everything necessary to sustain human life is at your local Office Depot. It should also be pointed out that Office Depot sells gift cards for just about anything else you will need throughout your life.

As the purchasing agent for his company, Stephan realized that the local Office Depot was a gold mine. Stephan would visit the store about three times per week. Over the course of a month, he would incur charges of about $4,000. When it came time to pay the Office Depot bill each month, the authorized check signer would see the face of the Office Depot statement, agree the amount on the statement to the check amount, sign the check, and then move on. Why did the check signer pay so little attention to the Office Depot statement? Because it is for office supplies, and everyone needs office supplies. No actual documentation was provided, no receipts, just the face of the statement reflecting the amount due. Because no further documentation was required, Stephan was able to purchase personal items undetected. The investigation showed that approximately 80 percent of the charges should have been classified as personal.

This and many similar stories about investigations I have performed over the years will make you a believer in the importance of documentation.

Sample Documentation

Receipts and Invoices   Receipts and invoices supporting cash and credit or debit card usage *must* accompany the monthly required expense report. The receipts and invoices should be attached to an 8½-by-11 piece of paper, which is then attached to the expense report. Sufficient description should be provided on the attachment to assist the accounting department in coding the charge to the proper general ledger account.

Supplemental Documentation for Business Meal and Entertainment Expense Charges   A separate supplemental business meal and entertainment charges form will be completed for each charge. This form requires the following documentation:

- Payee (establishment)
- Amount
- How paid
- Classification as meal or entertainment
- Date

- Time
- Name(s) of attendee(s)
- Business purpose
- Business relationship between the employee(s) and the guest(s)
- Signature of the responsible employee attendee

All of these charges must be accompanied by original receipts stapled to an 8½-by-11 piece of paper. Receipts must include *both* the itemized food and beverage receipt and the payment receipt (including gratuity).

The expense report form and, if applicable, the supplemental business meal and entertainment expense charges form must be submitted to and approved by the preparer's supervisor. Management's forms must be approved by the owner or a member of the board of directors.

Failure to follow these documentation requirements will result in the employee being required to reimburse the company for the charge.

This element of the policy requires the use of two forms, the expense report form and the supplemental business meal and entertainment charges form, as presented in Appendixes A and B to this chapter.

The information included on the expense report form solicits everything necessary for compliance with the documentation requirements of the policy. The layout of this form is straightforward and allows easy tracking, by day, of the expense incurred and the general ledger account to charge. The "paid with" column leaves no question as to whether the charge was paid with cash, credit card, or debit card. The far right column requires a check mark noting that the receipt is attached. A missing check mark in this column represents a charge that will be subject to reimbursement to the company by the employee.

The supplemental business meal and entertainment charges form is required for any charges noted in either the meals or entertainment columns of the expense report form. The form solicits the information necessary to comply with the additional documentation requirements of the policy.

Element 7. Statement of Responsibility

- Establishes that the employee understands the purpose of the policy, has read the policy, and agrees to abide by the terms of the policy.

Comments: Notice that the policy is intended not only to protect the company but also to protect the employee from financial hardship. This means that the company recognizes that if it opens up its credit to the use of employees without a reliable policy in place, the door is wide open for abuse. If the opportunity is not present, it simply can't happen.

Sample Statement of Responsibility

The use of the company-issued credit or debit card is an important privilege intended to facilitate business by the company. Adherence to this policy is vital not only in ensuring the continuation of this privilege but also in ensuring that neither you nor the company is subjected to financial hardship or public criticism.

I, _____, have read and understand the responsibilities outlined in this policy. I agree to abide by the provisions in this policy, and understand that violations of this policy could result in disciplinary actions including termination.

_____   _____
Signature   Date

The variations available to perform expense reimbursement fraud are actually unlimited. Every time I think I have seen it all, another slightly different case presents itself, and I start all over again trying to determine what clever device this person used.

At first glance, it may appear that the record-keeping processes and documentation requirements of this policy are overly time-consuming and burdensome. However, my experience has shown that operating within this policy ultimately saves you more time and money than can be measured. If it takes time to accumulate, review, and pay on the documentation, it takes more time to deal with the police, fraud examiners, attorneys, and trials associated with prosecuting the fraud. If it takes money to comply with this policy, it takes much more to pay the fraud examiners and attorneys to investigate and prosecute the fraud, not to mention the filing of insurance claims and payment of deductibles for recovery of the fraud loss.

There simply is no way to overstate the importance of including this policy in your anti-fraud program.

APPENDIX 4A: EXPENSE REPORT FORM

Month: September   Employee: Jeff Smith

Day	Payee	Lodging	Meals	Entertain-ment	Other Travel Description	GL Acct #	Amount	Other Expense Description	GL Acct #	Amount	Grand Total	Paid with	Receipt
1	The Omni	226.15									226.15	Credit Card	✓
1	Red Lobster		43.21								43.21	Cash	✓
2	Yellow Cab				Cab Fare	400.201	18.00				18.00	Cash	✓
4	Delta Airlines				Air Fare	400.201	396.76				396.76	Credit Card	✓
4	The Omni				Copies	500.300	9.00				9.00	Credit Card	✓
5	Office Depot							Manila Folders	501.000	14.15	14.15	Debit Card	✓
		226.15	43.21	0.00			423.76			14.15	707.27		

General Ledger Account **400.201** **400.300** **400.300**   **Travel Exp** **400.201** 414.76   **Office Supplies** 14.15   Cash Advance 100.00
      Travel Exp. **Meals & Ent** **Meals & Ent**   **500.300** 9.00   **501.000**   Cash Used (61.21)
                     423.76   Due from Employee 38.79

Employee Signature _____

Date _____

Approval Signature _____

Date _____

FIGURE 4A.1 Expense Report Form

APPENDIX 4B: SUPPLEMENTAL BUSINESS MEAL AND ENTERTAINMENT CHARGES FORM

Payee: Red Lobster	Explanation of Business Purpose:
Amount: 43.21 Cash	Met over dinner to review contract details
	and make final amendments
Classification: Meal	
Date: 9/1/20xx	
Time: 8:00pm	
Place: Nashville, Tennessee	
	Business Relationship between
Name(s) of Attendee(s):	Employee(s) and Guest(s):
Jeff Smith	Company Employee
John Clarke	Non-Company Contractor

Verification of Responsible Employee Attendee: (Signature) _____

1. To be completed when charging or reimbursing for meal and entertainment expenses.

2. All expenses that are submitted must be accompanied by original receipts taped to an 8 1/2" x 11" piece of paper. Receipts must include both the itemized food and beverage receipt and the payment receipt (including gratuity).

FIGURE 4B.2 Supplemental Business Meal and Entertainment Charges Form

CHAPTER FIVE

The Ground Floor

The Fraud Risk Assessment Process

Aftern Implementing the foundational policies of a sound anti-fraud environment, we can begin erecting the structure of the anti-fraud program. We will begin by laying the floor on the foundation.

My hobbies include home remodeling. I enjoy being able to envision a project from inception to completion and then live in the fruits of my labor. There are certain aspects of remodeling a home that I prefer over others. Laying the floor, whether with tile or hardwood, is the aspect I least enjoy. There are many small wooden planks involved in covering a thousand-square-foot area. When beginning that process, I am overwhelmed. All of the planks have to fit just right. An error early in the process reflects significantly at the end of the project. Similarly, the fraud risk assessment process can be a lot like laying a hardwood floor—an overwhelming task. The majority of frustration comes from not knowing how to think through the process. Additionally, once the thought process is sound, the documentation of the assessment takes over as a source of frustration. "I don't even want to start because I'm afraid of making a mistake early that will render my work useless." I hear that statement often.

The objective of this chapter is to calm the overwhelming fears that are so common in performing a fraud risk assessment. We are working on the ground floor, so let's establish some ground rules—pun intended.

GROUND RULES FOR FRAUD RISK ASSESSMENT

Rule 1. Don't Be Misled; It's Not as Hard as It Seems

Throughout my career, I have witnessed the birth of the simple fraud risk assessment process up to today's process packed with requirements for the completion of charts and checklists that would leave even the hard-core risk assessment enthusiast numb. Remember, we are attempting to get back to the basics. Let's strip away the complexities of the process and understand that it simply doesn't have to be that hard.

Rule 2. Place What You Know on the Back Burner, and Think the Unthinkable

This entire process focuses on asking, "If I were going to steal from my company or misstate my financial statements, how would I do it? What areas do I see as the easiest points of attack?" In doing this, I need to place my everyday concerns about running my business on the back burner and venture into areas I probably haven't even considered. The ability to think the unthinkable is critical to the success of the assessment.

Rule 3. Whether You Like It or Not, You Have to Think Like a Criminal

This ground rule speaks to the issue I deal with constantly as I teach fraud prevention courses. If I am going to teach you how to prevent fraud, I basically have to teach you how to commit fraud. While I don't desire that anyone become an expert, it must be understood that the ability to think like a criminal will result in the best overall coverage for your anti-fraud program.

Rule 4. Don't Overdocument the Process

This aspect may lead to the most fear in undertaking this process. We can work ourselves into a nervous frenzy with the thoughts of all of these meetings, all of these discussions, all of these ideas and possibilities, the first draft, the second draft, and on and on. It doesn't have to be and shouldn't be that way. An underlying principle in fraud risk assessment is that the process is intended to *identify* the risks. The development of control activities, the next section of this book, represents the process of preparing a *response* to those identified risks.

AN EXAMPLE OF RISK ASSESSMENT

Before we describe the semantics of performing a risk assessment, let's look at an example of a risk assessment issue for a financial institution.

Merebank is a relatively small bank with $150 million in total assets. The bank provides the normal range of lending services and provides checking accounts and various types of savings accounts for its customers. The bank has three teller drawer stations in the lobby and two teller stations at its drive-through. Each teller drawer contains a $2,500 normal established balance. The lending department includes one overworked loan officer and two loan-processing clerks.

When considering these two aspects of operations, how do we assess the risk of fraud? Let's begin by determining what internal controls are in place for the teller drawers. Only one teller can work out of an assigned drawer; that's good. Teller drawers are locked in the vault at night and require two people to access the vault each morning to get the respective teller drawers; that's good. End-of-day balancing procedures for each drawer require cross-verification with all daily work; that's good. If each teller decides to steal all of their teller cash, the bank loses a total of $12,500 that day.

The lending department is a different story. Per the assumptions presented here, the bank has only one loan officer. Obviously, this loan officer is over-worked and thus susceptible to not only errors in the paperwork but also errors in judgment. All lending authority is placed in this one lending position. When discussing other controls related to this area, the risk assessment team can't think of any existing internal controls. There is no secondary approval, there are no approval limits, there is no loan committee, and there are no loan review audit procedures in place.

So where is the fraud risk? It's not hard to determine; it's common sense. Teller controls are good. Lending controls aren't. One fictitious loan for $20,000 exceeds the loss from the theft of every dime in all of the teller drawers. Two fictitious loans for $20,000 each significantly exceed any teller drawer losses. So the risk assessment results in fraud risks identified in the lending area. While errors in the paperwork and errors in judgment (lending money when the borrower does not qualify) are possible and even probable, these issues are not fraud. So how can the loan officer steal from the bank? "Hmm, I will have to think like a criminal": Maybe I can disburse a loan to my father or in my father's name with the proceeds going to my account. Or I could just lend to a shell company (owned by me), not make any payments, and perform file maintenance on my loan each month by advancing the due date so my loan never becomes delinquent. I could go on and on. In reviewing our identified risks, we see that when we get to the point of designing internal controls, we will focus our control activities design on risks related to the lending area of our bank. This example illustrates the type of thought process necessary to accomplish an effective fraud risk assessment.

PROCEDURAL STEPS FOR PERFORMING A FRAUD RISK ASSESSMENT

Understand the Guiding Principles

Certain guiding principles must be understood at the beginning of the process:

1. There is no standard form, no one-size-fits-all fraud risk assessment process. Due to industry differences, organization size differences, and differences in products offered by similar organizations, there just simply cannot be a model or form that can be completed that properly addresses all vulnerabilities to fraud in organizations. It has even been said that fraud risk assessment is really more of an art than a science.
2. Fraud risk constantly changes because the operations of an organization constantly change. As a result, the process of fraud risk assessment is never really finished. Yes, we will get to the point in this book that we have completed and documented the assessment. But we have to understand that this process will undergo constant revision from that point forward.
3. The objective of the process is not to prevent fraud. The objective is to determine what frauds need to be prevented.

Determine the Participants

Some risk assessments are performed by one person, as in the case of a small organization with a manager and another employee or two. Other risk assessments are performed by a team of employees or committees. In organizations large enough to include a risk assessment team, the makeup of the team is critical. Again, a general guiding thought is that the team should include a representative from each operational area of the organization. Representatives from upper management, middle management, sales, accounting, human resources, legal, and billing are examples of the diversity that should exist on the risk assessment team. From this group, a facilitator should be selected. The facilitator does nothing more than guide the process and keep it on track. In no circumstance should the facilitator be viewed as a dictator.

Determine How Information Will Be Gathered

This procedural step is where I differ most from others in the approach to performing a fraud risk assessment. There are numerous ways to solicit and gather information for the risk assessment. Do we establish focus groups, do we interview everyone in the organization, do we seek anonymous input, or do we send out surveys? What about a combination of all of these?

Remember, the motto of this book is a return to *simple practicality.* These methods of gathering information are all effective, but they tend to foster those feelings of being overwhelmed. I have to admit that I am not a meeting guy. I have witnessed significant productivity declines from having too many meetings to discuss productivity. When I am asked to help an organization with anti-fraud program design, and I can't even get started because this employee or that employee is constantly tied up in meetings, I get a good feeling about where the first change will be recommended. Stop meeting and start working! However, this meeting, the fraud risk assessment meeting, is one that I certainly endorse.

Let me state again that I have no issue with those methods. They are all effective. However, focus groups involve a lot of meetings, interviews obviously result in more meetings, and surveys significantly increase the number of meetings. Someone has to design the survey and then summarize the results, which represent more meetings, more meetings, and more meetings. Therefore, my approach to gathering information is based on simple practicality and the desire to follow the ground rule that it doesn't have to be this hard.

What is my approach? Well, it can be outlined as follows:

- Gather the team.
- Go into this room.
- Talk.
- Have someone write down what is said.

How do we talk about what we need to talk about? Following this structure significantly simplifies the process.

Identify Areas of Fraud Risk

I like to begin by looking at two of the basic financial statements of every organization: the balance sheet and the income statement. If you think about it, every line item or category on the financial statements represents an area we need to assess. Most balance sheets begin with line items like cash in bank, accounts receivable, and inventory. Income statements begin with line items like sales and expenses. If the only three line items on a balance sheet were those referenced here, my approach would be to ask, "What is the fraud risk associated with cash in bank, then accounts receivable, then inventory?" Financial statements provide the outline of areas that should be addressed. The team didn't have to prepare the financial statements; they already exist. Let's use them to our advantage. In doing so, we avoid the pitfall of reinventing the wheel to begin our assessment process.

At this point, we can begin to ask the three questions that I consider necessary to properly perform the assessment. These three questions encompass everything we are trying to accomplish in a risk assessment.

1. **Identify the risk.** How can someone steal from us or misstate this line item?
2. **Establish the initial priority of the risk.** How likely do we think it is that this could occur?
3. **Quantify the risk and establish its final priority.** How would it affect the organization financially if it did occur?

Once the risks have been identified and prioritized, we can then *address* the risks and decide what our response will be. What control activities will we establish?

To better answer the first question, a review of the three types of fraud is necessary.

1. **Asset misappropriation:** Taking company assets can be accomplished through cash frauds, such as skimming and check fraud, or through non-cash frauds, such as theft or abuse of inventory or trade secrets.
2. **Corruption:** Collusion between at least two individuals can be accomplished through bribery, kickbacks, bid rigging, and illegal gratuities.
3. **Financial statement fraud:** Intentional misstatement of financial statements for varying purposes could involve making the numbers look worse than reality, possibly for tax savings purposes, or making the numbers look better, possibly for debt covenant compliance purposes.

With this base understanding in place, we can begin an example of risk assessment for Scotco, Inc., based on the balance sheet included in Figure 5.1. This example is certainly not all-inclusive. The intent is to illustrate the thought processes necessary in performing the risk assessment. The numbers presented in the financial statements are small-dollar numbers for ease of presentation.

SCOTCO, Inc.
Balance Sheet
As of December 31, 20XX

Assets

Current Assets:

Cash in Bank	$	15,624
Customer Accounts Receivable		11,991
Less: Allowance for Uncollectible Accounts		(1,052)
Employee Accounts Receivable		4,819
Investments		25,000
Inventory—Merchandise		14,621
	$	71,003

Noncurrent Assets:

Long-Term Investments	$	145,000

Depreciable Fixed Assets:

Land	$	16,000
Depreciable Fixed Assets		188,600
Less: Accumulated Depreciation		(44,644)
	$	143,956
Total Assets	$	359,959

Liabilities

Current Liabilities:

Accounts Payable	$	16,320
Payroll Taxes Payable		2,822
Other Current Liabilities		9,438
	$	28,580

Shareholders' Equity

Common Stock: ($1 Par Value; 100,000 Shares Authorized; 50,000 Shares Issued and Outstanding)	$	50,000
Additional Paid-in-Capital		150,000
Retained Earnings		131,379
	$	331,379
Total Liabilities and Shareholders' Equity	$	359,959

FIGURE 5.1 Balance Sheet

The information that follows is presented in a conversational format. Remember, we have called our team into the room to talk, and someone is writing it all down on paper. The conversation begins with the first line item on the financial statement.

 ## CASH IN BANK

Lane (the Manager): "The first line item I see here is Cash in Bank. That line item includes our main operating bank account and the payroll bank account. So how could someone steal from these accounts?"

Micah (the Accounting Supervisor): "Well, I know that the senior accountant is responsible for reconciling the bank accounts. She also has the ability to collect accounts receivable payments and post to the customer accounts, as well as the ability to post general journal entries to the general ledger. I suppose she could record a false deposit into the bank account with the offsetting credit being used to reduce her employee account receivable balance. She could do all of this through a general journal entry. Since she reconciles the accounts, she could alter the balance per bank on the bank reconciliation to conceal the fraud."

Lane: "Well, that was easy. It looks like we have some work to do."

Allan (a Warehouseman): "Our bank accounts include all of the company funds, so really any attack that reduces this bank account through fraud should be looked at."

Micah: "Yes, just think about our monthly travel or business expense reimbursement process. Our employees are required to complete a monthly expense report and attach the supporting documentation with the checks to be signed. But is anyone really looking at and verifying all of that documentation before signing the check?"

Lane: "That is my responsibility, and I have to admit that sometimes I don't look through *all* of the documentation religiously. Some days I'm buried in paperwork, and some days I'm not. So what can we do about this?"

Micah: "Well, let's see here. We have identified a segregation of duties problem with the senior accountant position, and we also have a validation problem in the check signing area."

At this point in the example, we need to consider how to document what has surfaced in this conversation. To provide a guideline, consider Figure 5.2, a simple, practical form that can be used to document this short conversation.

Identified Fraud Risks and Schemes	Likelihood	Financial Significance	Risk Ref. No.
Misappropriation of Assets:			
Bank reconciliations are performed by a position that has the ability to collect payments and post to accounts receivable, as well as the ability to post general journal entries to the ledger. This is a segregation of duties problem that could result in:			
1. Posting false deposits into the bank account to reduce employee accounts receivable balances.	With all of this control, it is very likely that numerous types of fraud could occur.	Unlimited. This is the entry and exit point of all of the company funds.	1
The travel and business expense reimbursement system in place is okay, but management admits that not all of the documentation is reviewed before signing the checks. This could result in:			
1. Employees claiming reimbursement for false or fictiticus items.	With the validation process not being adhered to very well, the likelihood of a false reimbursement request is high.	This seems like an opportunity for a quick take, not necessarily in large dollar amounts. Anything very large is going to show up in our expense accounts fairly quickly.	2

FIGURE 5.2 Fraud Risk Assessment Framework

Please note the simplicity of this form. From left to right, the columns represent the three questions of the risk assessment process. The fourth column is to provide a reference number for the identified fraud risks that must be addressed when designing the *control activities*, which is the next section of this book.

There are no benchmarks such as, on a scale of 1 to 10, what is the likelihood of occurrence? That overcomplicates the process. This process should be documented with commonsense talk that we use in real life.

Also notice that we did not document the conversation verbatim like a court reporter. We simply put on paper the risks that came from that conversation. As we delve deeper into the risk assessment process, we constantly focus on the first question: How can someone steal from us?

The following case investigations may shed further insight into the various ways employees can steal.

 ## CASE: THE TRAIL IS GONE

Reva, an accounts payable clerk, cost her company on average $3,000 per month over a three-year period by charging personal expenses to the company credit card. In all honesty, this fraud isn't anything new. This exact fraud has been occurring for years. Reva perpetrated and concealed this fraud quite easily by signing up for the paperless statement delivery option and the new, convenient online bill-paying system.

Why is allowing those options so flawed? Let's consider the same scenario under a system without the paperless statement option or the online bill-paying option. The old accounts payable system includes a purchase order, a receiving slip, and an invoice. The mail is opened by someone who logs the incoming contents under dual control and then distributes those invoices to the employee responsible for approving them. That employee then reviews all of the documentation and approves the invoice for payment. Only when the invoices are approved for payment, the accounts payable department prepares the check and attaches the supporting documentation to the check. All of this is then forwarded to the individual responsible for signing the check, who is required to examine the supporting documentation for validity. Once satisfied with the validity of the documentation, the individual responsible for signing the check signs it. The check and supporting documentation are sent back to accounting for mailing the check and filing the paperwork. There it is, the perfect accounts payable disbursement system.

Reva figured it out. If there is no invoice and no check, I can completely remove the trail of this disbursement from this long, convoluted, and sound internal control process. What appears convenient and efficient at first actually makes fraud incredibly easy to commit and easy to overlook.

CASE: FRIENDS IN LOW PLACES

Ron, the warehouseman for his company, colluded with an outside supplier to add to his personal net worth. Ron returned worn truck tires to the supplier and received a credit toward the purchase of new tires. However, the supplier established a separate credit, or rebate account, funded by the credits applied to the tires returned by Ron. Ron's company never received the benefit of the credits; this separate account at the supplier did. Then Ron and the supplier employee split the amount in this separate credit account. The 50-50 kickback made both of them relatively wealthy.

These two examples represent a glimpse into how employees steal from their organizations. The examples could go on and on. Sadly, theft is limited only by imagination.

Returning to our risk assessment process, we have our team in the room and are going down the line items on the financial statements to ask the three risk assessment questions of each. Identified risks are included on the fraud risk assessment framework form. This information will be used to develop the specific *control activities* to address these risks. That's it; that's the process. It's not hard; it's not overly documented. It is simply the process of talking and thinking outside our normal comfort zones. Depending on your company's complexity level, this fraud risk assessment framework form may be 2 pages long or 50 pages long. Whatever the length, this is your documented risk assessment.

These discussions branch into how the line items could be misstated for financial statement fraud. The stealing questions result in thinking about how assets can be misappropriated or how corruption can be performed in these various areas. Some level of fraud education is necessary in every organization to keep these conversations focused and productive.

The case examples in this chapter scratch the surface of considering the ways employees can commit fraud. The information that follows provides an outline of the various types of schemes that exist within each type of fraud. This information is available from many sources but is most effectively summarized and presented in the Association of Certified Fraud Examiners' *Report to the Nations on Occupational Fraud and Abuse.* A free copy of this report can be obtained from its website at www.acfe.com. This document provides additional information regarding each specific scheme noted here.

Additionally, as we move into the development of *control activities* section of this book, we will delve deeper into the specifics of a majority of these schemes.

For purposes of presentation, this information is summarized according to the three types of fraud.

 ## ASSET MISAPPROPRIATION

This type of fraud includes two categories: cash fraud and noncash fraud (inventory and all other assets).

Cash fraud can be further divided into three categories:

1. **Theft of cash on hand:** This is relatively straightforward in that the employee steals the cash directly from the change drawer or the petty cash fund. I have investigated cash thefts ranging from $25 out of the petty cash fund to over a million dollars, all at one time, from vault cash at a financial institution.
2. **Theft of cash receipts:** As related to this type of theft, an important distinction must be understood. Cash larceny represents cash that is stolen from the organization after having already been recorded in the records. Skimming represents cash that is stolen from the organization before it is recorded. Skimming schemes include the following:
   ▪ Sales (unrecorded or understated)
   ▪ Receivables (lapping or write-off schemes)
   ▪ Refunds and other
3. **Fraudulent disbursements:** These schemes keep me the busiest. Without them, I'm not sure I could keep my business operating. This category is further subcategorized as follows:

   Billing Schemes
   ▪ Shell companies
   ▪ Nonaccomplice vendor
   ▪ Personal purchases

   Payroll Schemes
   ▪ Ghost employees
   ▪ Falsified wages
   ▪ Commission schemes

Expense Reimbursement Schemes
- Mischaracterized expenses
- Overstated expenses
- Fictitious expenses
- Multiple reimbursements

Check Tampering
- Forged maker
- Forged endorsement
- Altered payee
- Authorized maker

Register Disbursements
- False voids
- False refunds

Noncash fraud includes frauds perpetrated on inventory and other assets. These fraud schemes are evidenced by misuse and larceny.

 ## CORRUPTION

The corruption type of fraud has the following four subcategories:

1. **Conflicts of interest:** Usually present in purchases and sales schemes.
2. **Bribery:** Kickbacks and bid-rigging schemes.
3. **Illegal gratuities:** These can include items that are limited only by one's imagination, such as vacations, athletic event tickets, and sexual favors.
4. **Economic extortion:** This involves a threat such as "I'll do business with you as long as you do business with my side company."

 ## FINANCIAL STATEMENT FRAUD

This type of fraud can be specified in two ways:

1. Asset or revenue overstatements, which can be further categorized as:
   - Timing differences
   - Fictitious revenues

- Concealed liabilities and expenses
- Improper asset valuations
- Improper disclosures
2. Asset or revenue understatements, which can be further categorized as:
   - Timing differences
   - Understated revenues
   - Overstated liabilities and expenses
   - Improper asset valuations

•　•　•

As you go through this process of fraud risk assessment, the guiding principles presented in this chapter will help you keep that overwhelmed feeling at bay. It doesn't have to be that hard, just common sense.

PART TWO

Anti-Fraud Control Activities: Raising the Walls

THE DESIGN OF CONTROL activities is a critical stage in the development of the anti-fraud program. If you were to review the anti-fraud programs of two companies, this area would contain the majority of differences in the overall programs because companies differ in size, industry, and complexity of operations. The lack of a one-size-fits-all model is most evident in this part.

Without personally working with your business, I cannot provide you with all of your unique and necessary control activities, but I have provided you with a simple method to understand your own needs.

The chapters included in Part II address the major differences that can be encountered in designing control activities through the presentation of the following topics:

- The absolute control activities that should be included in every anti-fraud program regardless of these differences.
- Control activities that can be implemented when segregation of duties is impossible.

This part also addresses the fact that certain control activities should be designed for transaction processes, and certain activities need to be designed for specific financial statement line item areas.

CHAPTER SIX

Control Activities

The Absolutes

YOU HAVE COMPLETED a thorough risk assessment. What now? It does no good if you simply know the risks. You have to do something about them. You have to respond to them. Developing specific control activities is the response to the identified fraud risks.

Similar to the fraud risk assessment, this process can seem somewhat overwhelming. However, common sense should prevail, and common sense should keep it simple.

These absolute strategies discuss an approach to developing and documenting the control activities that make up the core of the anti-fraud program. To begin the process of control activities design, several critical principles *must* be understood.

 ## CRITICAL PRINCIPLES OF CONTROL ACTIVITY DESIGN

Principle 1. Design the Internal Control around the *Position*, Never around the *Person* in That Position

This is the critical principle of internal control design. People always change, but the position most likely does not. Take an accountant position as an example. Natalie has been the company accountant for the past 20 years. The company is expecting her retirement soon; unfortunately, she will be gone sooner than we think. You see, today just isn't her day. She just stepped in front of the proverbial bus while leaving the office. So now you have the same accounting position but a different person serving in that position. Natalie was honest. She would never take a dime, so you really weren't that concerned about the internal controls in her area. But the new accountant, Michael, is a crook. He is now set up to be the beneficiary of her honesty. If only the company had established controls for the accountant position, they wouldn't now be vulnerable to the accountant person.

Remember that 95 percent of those I have investigated are truly decent people who rationalize their fraud because of a severe financial crisis. They are able to take advantage of the company simply because their position has weak internal controls. Believing you don't need internal controls because you don't have evil people working for you is irrelevant. Evil people don't represent the majority of fraud instances; desperate people do. Even if you don't accept this reality, placing your faith in people's honesty still leaves you vulnerable. Five percent of those I have investigated steal for greed or other evil motivations and are not detected until the crime has already been committed.

Principle 2. The Perception of Detection Is the Strongest Internal Control That Can Be Implemented

There is an immeasurable strengthening in an anti-fraud program when the perception of detection increases. I am often asked to assist companies with establishing their initial internal audit function. I let them know up front that the process of properly establishing this function from scratch takes approximately three years. However, before they lose hope, I quickly let them know that it can immediately be effective for prevention purposes.

Immediate prevention is possible because the workforce knows that an internal audit function is being established. They know this because you told them in your periodic fraud awareness and prevention training. Right away, they know that someone is now watching. That, in and of itself, is enough to increase the perception of detection. People who know they may be caught may not go through with the planned fraud. The numerous procedures or processes that will be audited on a periodic basis, the internal audit work plan, should be communicated to the workforce in the periodic training sessions. Obviously, you should not communicate the length of time needed to get up to speed. Even if it really is three years before the new controls are firmly established, the immediate knowledge of a plan is a major fraud deterrent.

If your organization is not large enough to consider establishing an internal audit department, there are still control activities to implement that will increase the perception of detection. Every company can benefit from implementing the foundational control activities, the absolutes.

 ## FOUNDATIONAL CONTROL ACTIVITIES

There is no one-size-fits-all anti-fraud program, but there are control activities that should be included in each one. Even though organizations reflect differences in industry, size, products or services, and operational complexity, I believe every organization should have some basic internal controls. I have defined certain control activities as foundational because I have repeatedly experienced breakdowns in these same controls that, had they been in place, there would have been nothing to investigate. For every case I investigate, I make an assessment of missing controls and/or determine existing controls that were not followed that resulted in the perpetrator being able to commit and conceal the fraud. Time after time, it seems that the same weaknesses or breakdowns led to the fraud. These foundational controls are presented here, categorized according to the design elements of an effective anti-fraud program.

Anti-Fraud Environment

The fraud, fraud reporting, and expense reimbursement policies have previously been presented in detail in Chapters 2 through 4, respectively. I simply reiterate because these foundational policies have to be included in any anti-fraud program.

> **Organization chart:** I have consulted with too many organizations whose employees simply did not know who was in charge. As difficult as this is to conceive, it is all too common. An organization chart lends support to an anti-fraud program because it specifically defines the authority levels and chain of command.
>
> **Formal written job descriptions for all positions:** An employee without a formal job description is at the mercy of whoever is in their presence at the moment. "Betty is telling me to do one thing, Mark is telling me to do another, and Clark is telling me to do the same thing as Betty but in a different way." The organization chart provides an answer to part of this issue by defining the proper chain of authority, and a job description further defines the employee's specific duties. Lack

of productivity and low morale are a by-product of employees who do not know what their jobs functions include. I have witnessed dramatic increases in morale and productivity as organizations establish formal job descriptions. The positive effects simply cannot be measured.

Employee evaluations: An overstressed, angry workforce leads to increased opportunities for employees to rationalize their way into committing fraud. Common rationalizations of an angry workforce include feelings like:

"I didn't get the raise or promotion I deserve, so I will just take it."
"It's not fair. Ron did the same thing and no one said a word."
"Management does it, my coworkers do it, so why shouldn't I?"

Annual employee evaluations provide the opportunity for individual employees to know where they stand regarding the perceived quality of their work. Evaluations also provide the employee with areas of job performance that they can work to improve. If employees are not evaluated and corrected, there is no chance for them to improve. Employees who are given an annual evaluation feel that management cares about them and their development. This not only fosters a better team atmosphere but also serves to reduce the risk of an angry rationalization.

Employee payroll advance and financial counseling programs: In Larry's case, outside financial pressures led him to commit fraud. Larry's company had no programs from which he could seek a payroll advance or obtain some type of financial counseling to get past his personal financial crisis. As a result, Larry felt he had no place to turn. The availability of these types of programs can reduce the incentives or pressures for an employee to even consider committing a fraudulent act.

Required employee dishonesty insurance and fidelity bonds: A strong anti-fraud environment includes a governing body or ownership-management team that understands the importance of fraud awareness and prevention. Part of this understanding is the awareness that, regardless of the best prevention efforts, losses from fraud may occur and thus need to be insured through proper employee dishonesty insurance or fidelity bond insurance. This type of insurance should be considered an absolute necessity for business continuation purposes.

Fraud Risk Assessment

Requirement to perform: The required performance of a fraud risk assessment is obviously one of the primary issues covered in this book. This requirement itself is a control activity.

Control Activities

Preemployment background and reference checks: I received a call recently from the U.S. Secret Service wanting the case file for a fraud investigation that I had performed six years in the past. This case had been tried, the defendant convicted, and the sentence served. On release from prison, the convicted woman obtained employment with a company literally across the street from the company she defrauded. I asked the Secret Service agent why he needed the file. He told me that she went across the street to this new job and committed the same type of fraud. No background or reference checks had ever been performed. This simple control activity could have prevented much pain and heartache for this second employer.

I often am asked, "Why should I perform reference checks since no one included on an applicant's resume is going to say anything bad about the person?" I believe that reference checks are still useful. My personal experience has shown that often employees do not ask me if they may include me as a reference on their resume. I have received reference calls from potential employers for applicants that I had no idea included me as a reference. If they had known what was good for them, they never would have included me as a reference. Some of them are among the worst employees I have ever had. I can't imagine what they were thinking when they put me down as a reference. However, they did.

Obviously, I have to be extremely careful with the answers I provide. I verify employment dates and salaries with no problem. But then the bombshell question is asked: "If given the opportunity, would you rehire this individual?" Be careful; how you answer this question could get you in a fair amount of trouble. If I would rehire this person, I simply respond with yes. If I wouldn't rehire this person even as the last person on earth, I simply don't respond. As the old saying goes, silence is golden. A potential employer who cannot understand what my silence means probably deserves to hire this applicant.

Required annual completion of the conflict of interest form: This form solicits information from all employees, owners, and even members of the governing body about any familial, personal, business, or financial relationships with those outside the organization. The purpose of obtaining this information is to protect the organization and even its decision makers when considering with whom the organization does business and in matters such as awarding contracts. Conflicts of interest may arise when choosing an office supplies vendor if the board chairman's wife, son, or other close relation owns the office supply company. Possibly the chief executive officer owns the office supply company.

I recently investigated a contract procurement fraud case in which the chief executive officer's brother owned a construction company that was awarded a $22 million contract, incidentally as the lowest bid. Because this was a family deal, certain aspects of the bidder's lack of compliance with the minimum bid specification requirements was not brought to the attention of the other two members of the committee making the decision on awarding the contract. As soon as the construction activities began, the problems surfaced. There was no contractor bond, improper materials were being used, and so on. Without getting into the details, the project ended in complete disaster for the company, as well as for the brother's company.

Had the decision makers known that this bidder was the CEO's brother, a little more attention would hopefully have been given to the bid that the brother submitted, and the correct decision would have been made.

The required completion of the conflict of interest form is not only for contract procurement issues. It applies to all vendors providing any type of service or product to the organization. Chapter 8 presents the requirement for compliance with new vendor establishment procedures, which include obtaining information that is used to determine any potential conflicts of interest that may exist.

An example conflict of interest form is included as Appendix 6A to this chapter.

Required use of vacation time (at least five consecutive business days): This quite possibly is the oldest control activity in existence. It must have stood the test of time because it is that good. For morale and productivity, it is always good for employees to be able to take a break, take a vacation, and refresh themselves. Additionally, it is an outstanding control activity. At least a full business week should be required to be taken at one time. A five-day absence makes it extremely difficult for the perpetrator to keep the fraud concealed. Either the fraud falls out during that time period, or someone has to perform the duties of the vacationing employee and therefore detects the fraud while performing these duties.

Required supporting documentation and approval for nonstandard journal entries: I recently investigated a fraud case where an employee reduced her employee accounts receivable balance significantly by recording journal entries to credit her accounts receivable with the offsetting debit posted as a false deposit to the company bank account. She was also the individual responsible for performing the monthly bank reconciliation, so she could easily alter the balance per the bank on the bank reconciliation. With no requirement to provide supporting documentation and no requirement for approval of the journal entry, she could easily perpetrate the fraud. The addition of this simple control activity would have rendered this fraud impossible.

Annual physical inventory count: This control activity almost seems like a waste of time to include in this book. Everyone knows this is a necessary business process and a necessary control activity. However, I am constantly amazed at how many organizations do not perform this simple process. Inventory theft could be concealed forever if a comparison between what the records say is there and what is really there is never performed.

Governing body or owner approval of inventory write-offs: To conceal an inventory theft, the perpetrator often records a journal entry to write off the amount stolen. When proper approval of the write-off is not required, the theft can go undetected for an extended period of time.

Governing body or owner approval of charge-offs of accounts receivable and/or debit balance accounts payable: Charge-offs of accounts receivable balances are simplified when there is no requirement that the charge-off be reviewed and approved by the proper authority, usually the governing body or owner of the organization. I have seen numerous times in financial institutions where a fictitious loan is made and then charged off with no knowledge by anyone of the fraudulent act. This same principle is true with debit balance accounts payable items.

Required approval for billing adjustments or other credits to accounts receivable accounts: In the majority of organizations I work with, the ability to record a billing adjustment or some other type of nonrecurring credit to an accounts receivable account is quite simple. I often see employee accounts or an employee's friend or family account reduced in this manner. The amounts are small, so concealment of the fraud is easy. Billing adjustments and other credits should be required to have a supervisor level of review and approval before being recorded.

Required completion and validation of the information on the new vendor establishment form: One of the most common areas of fraud in any organization is known as the shell company fraud.

CASE: THE MAIL DROP IN LAS VEGAS

Ryan was the purchasing agent for his employer, an electric utility company that provided electricity to its customers in a 15-county area in the southwestern United States. High-dollar electric transformers were a constant need for the company to be able to provide the service to its customers.

Ryan perpetrated the textbook shell company scheme by creating a fictitious company, RTP, Inc. Ryan created fictitious invoices from RTP for electric transformers and submitted them to his employer for payment. Ryan had subscribed to a mail drop in Las Vegas, Nevada, to use as the remittance address for payments to RTP. The mail drop service then sent the payment to Ryan, who deposited the payment in a separate bank account established for this single purpose.

Ryan's problems began when an employee of the bank noticed that the address on the check did not match the address they had on record for Ryan, the account holder. The bank account holder's address was Ryan's home address. The employee of the bank put a hold on that check, called the electric company and inquired about that check, and informed management of the concerns. When informed of the account holder's name and address, management immediately knew it was Ryan, their employee. This fraud could have been perpetrated for a long time if not for the actions of the bank employee.

To avoid detection, the shell company is often given a name that is similar to an existing valid vendor. In this case, the valid vendor was Reynolds Transformer Production. The vendor master file of the electric company referred to this company as Reynolds Transformer Production, Inc., Reynolds, and RTP. Ryan established his shell company as RTP, Inc.

In an effort to reduce the probabilities of this type of scenario, proper vendor establishment procedures, including the following, should be placed in operation.

- Name: As reflected in state registration databases or organizational documents (articles of incorporation)
- Business reference name: If different from above
- Name: To be used as the payee
- Phone number
- Address
- Remittance address: If different from above
- Contact person

- Contact e-mail
- W-9 required: Taxpayer ID and type of business
- Disclosure of owner relationships to company personnel

This can be accomplished through the use of a form such as is presented as Appendix 6B to this chapter.

Once the information is obtained, processes need to be performed and documented that validate the information presented, such as phone calls to the number provided, e-mail to the e-mail address provided, Google searches, and state tax base searches.

Finally, the monitoring section of the anti-fraud program should include provisions for a periodic vendor master file audit to determine that vendors listed in the vendor master file have been subjected to these validation provisions.

> **Separate cashier or teller drawers for each employee:** Whether your organization is a bank or just has numerous cash drawers, separate teller or cash drawers must be required. Tellers and cashiers who can work out of numerous drawers are considered to have no internal control whatsoever around their positions. If a drawer is short, there is no way to determine who took the money.
>
> In smaller organizations where segregation of duties is not possible, it is best to design a control activity such as this to narrow the scope of employees who could have committed the fraud. In this example, if an employee steals from a cash drawer that several employees use, there is no ability to determine ultimate responsibility. Conversely, if one employee is responsible for that drawer, that employee is the prime suspect if a theft were to occur.
>
> **Checks will not be signed until all supporting documentation is verified or validated by the authorized check signer:** The individual with the responsibility to sign checks for the organization *has* to perform this function to its fullest extent. The authorized check signers should understand that they are to sign no check without the supporting documentation for that check (invoice, check request, purchase order, etc.) being attached to the check. The control also states that the authorized check signer should then, without fail, review the attached supporting documentation to determine that the purchase was for a valid business purpose, is properly supported, and is prepared in the correct amount. I have encountered numerous instances of fraud where

the authorized check signer was too busy to religiously look through all of that information. All it takes is one instance of a cursory glance, and the money is gone. Remember Larry's fraud? Lack of review of the supporting documentation led to Larry's ability to defraud his employer of $1.3 million.

Information: Program Documentation

Require a written anti-fraud program: Obviously, this control should be included in the anti-fraud program since this is the entire subject matter of this book. The requirement *for* the written program is included *in* the written program. So which comes first, the chicken or the egg? It doesn't matter. Whoever looks at the written program after you are long gone will quickly get the point that this is important to the overall safety of the organization.

Communication: The Company Fraud Training Program

Conduct continuous fraud awareness training: As discussed in Chapter 11, periodic, continuous fraud awareness and prevention training based around the contents of the anti-fraud program is an absolute. If the workforce has no awareness of the risks or costs of fraud, then the effectiveness of prevention efforts is nil.

Monitoring and Routine Maintenance

Periodic master vendor file audit: As stated in the control activity for new vendor establishment procedures, this is one of the controls that should absolutely be audited for compliance in the monitoring section. If compliance with this control does not exist, the financial risk is substantial.

Validation that check signing procedures are being followed: The audit for compliance with check signing procedures is another absolute. Lack of compliance with this control seems to be commonplace. I have investigated too many frauds that would not have happened had compliance with this control activity been adequate.

This list of absolute control activities represents those that I encounter most often as either missing or overridden. Their inclusion in the anti-fraud program will significantly reduce instances of fraud.

APPENDIX 6A: CONFLICT OF INTEREST FORM

SCOTCO, Inc
Conflict of Interest Form

To be completed annually by all employees, owners, and members of the governing body. If there are any questions as to what category a relationship should be included, select one and management shall determine any necessary reclassifications.

Name: _____

Title: _____   Signature: _____

Please provide individual names, company names, and the nature of the relationships that may exist with organizations that our company does business with or that you could reasonably expect our company to potentially enter into a relationship with, as relates to:

Family Relationships:

_____
_____
_____
_____

Personal Relationships:

_____
_____
_____
_____

Business Relationships:

_____
_____
_____
_____

Financial Relationships:

_____
_____
_____
_____

FIGURE 6A.1   Conflict of Interest Form

Your Company Name
New Vendor Establishment

Vendor Information		Validation Procedures				
		Documents or Procedures Performed				
Vendor Name:	ABC Company, Inc.	AOI	State Reg.	Googled		
Taxpayer ID#:	00-0000000	W-9				
Payee Name:	ABC Company					
Duplicate Name Search:		None Noted				
Primary Phone:	000-000-0000	Called—Active Number				
Fax No.:	000-000-0001	Test Fax Successful				
Website:	www.abc.aaa	Active				
Physical Address:		Googled—Valid			Google Earth—Valid	
Address:	1412 1st Street					
City:	City					
State:	State					
Zip Code:	11111					
Mailing Address:		Googled—Valid			Google Earth—Valid	
Address:	P.O. Box 9999					
City:	City					
State:	State					
Zip Code:	11111					
Duplicate Address Search:		None Noted				
Contact Person:	Jane Doe					
Contact E-mail:	jane@abc.aaa	E-mail to and from—Successful				

Expected Transactions:

Widget Purchases OR Monthly Statement Processing Services, etc.

Vendor Relationships:

Jane Doe is John Doe's sister. John works in our marketing department

FIGURE 6B.1 New Vendor Establishment Form

7

Control Activities

The Segregation of Duties Dilemma

 BUT I ONLY HAVE TWO EMPLOYEES

"Segregation of duties": I cannot possibly count the number of times I have heard or uttered these words during my career. So what is segregation of duties? The principles of segregation of duties state that no single individual or group of individuals should have the ability to commit and also conceal a fraud. The duties that should always be segregated for sound internal control purposes are

- Custody of assets
- Authorization or approval of transactions affecting those assets
- Recording or reporting those transactions

Depending on the complexity of operations and number of employees in an organization, the number of employees needed to ensure a proper segregation of duties may, and probably will, outweigh the resources available to pay all of these employees. It would be quite easy for me to recommend to all organizations that they need at least 10 individuals in their accounting department. However, that is certainly not practical.

Those organizations that have only two employees cannot properly segregate duties. Because of this fact, I often hear, "Well, I only have two employees so I don't need to worry about internal controls since it wouldn't do me any good anyway." To some extent, this statement is logical. But let me provide some hope. There is something we can do about this.

 ## PREVENTION VERSUS DETECTION CONTROLS

This book's purpose, a *prevention* focus, is to develop an effective anti-fraud program. It is not intended to be a fraud auditing book, which indicates a *detection* focus. Although some auditing issues are mentioned, they are mentioned in the context of auditing for compliance with following the control, not for detection of fraud.

However, in those organizations that lack the staff size necessary for proper segregation of duties, it becomes necessary to think along the lines of detection controls rather than prevention controls. The detection controls in this section are basic detection controls or review processes that should be performed when segregation of duties is not possible. The controls presented do not constitute a fraud audit and are not intended to result in a fraud audit. In fact, it may be easier to think of these detection controls as review processes. As we discuss the various processes that can be placed in operation, we must operate with the following basic understanding: Establishing detection controls, process reviews, is not necessarily for the purpose of fraud prevention, but rather is an attempt to reduce the amount of time before a fraud is detected.

It stands to reason that the longer a fraud goes undetected, the higher the dollar amount of the fraud. So while you may not prevent the fraud altogether, you can certainly reduce its effect on your organization.

In a story previously presented, the accountant recorded journal entries to credit her employee accounts receivable account, therefore reducing the amount she ultimately owed to her employer. The debit side to the journal entry was represented by a false deposit into the bank account. She also had the responsibility for performing the monthly bank reconciliations. To conceal the fraud, she altered the balance per the bank statement line item on the bank reconciliation to reflect a higher balance than what the bank statement actually reflected. Remember, she was recording false deposits, so she had to conceal this in some manner. As such, she had custody of the bank account, the ability to authorize transactions related to the bank account, and the ultimate recording and reporting of balances in the accounts receivable and bank accounts. There was no segregation of duties. She was the only employee in the accounting department.

The only process in place that even remotely resembled an internal control was the board of directors' review of the total page of the aged accounts receivable report. This was done each month in the board of directors' meeting. As part of my investigation, I obtained the board of directors' meeting minutes and looked at the total page of the aged accounts receivable report that they reviewed for a particular month. The report, though computer generated, showed crossed-out numbers replaced with handwritten numbers. Upon inquiry, the accountant told the board members that she wrote the new numbers on the report because there was a "timing difference." That's all, nothing else. No further questions asked. After all, they trusted her!

I know what you're saying. "Well, they were just careless and lazy." Maybe so, but trust me when I say that this is not a rare, isolated occurrence. This type of review process is more common than not.

Given the facts of this case, what could have been done to detect this fraud quicker? I offer the following:

- Implement a board review process of the complete aged accounts receivable report, not just the total page.
- Require documentation that supports any alterations to the information reviewed.
- Require a management or board member review of the bank reconciliation to compare the previous month's reconciliation to the current month's reconciliation. Look for outstanding checks that haven't cleared and deposits in transit that remain on the reconciliation from one month to the next. Obtain explanations for these uncleared items.
- Require that the accountant provide the bank reconciliation and the actual bank statement as part of the routine accounting documents that are reviewed in the board meeting each month. Compare the balance per the bank statement to the balance per the bank reconciliation, and obtain an explanation if these amounts are different (which they should never be).

This example illustrates the need to implement review processes that are aimed at detecting fraud. Whether the organization has a board of directors, a single owner, or multiple owners, the simple fact is that with the lack of ability to properly segregate duties, multiple review processes must be present.

THE NECESSARY REVIEW PROCESSES

Let's consider other review processes that should be implemented as presented in accordance with the line items on the basic set of financial statements. The terms *board member, board committee, owner,* and *manager* are used synonymously with the term *responsible party*. It is assumed that the balance sheet and income statement are already a part of the monthly information provided to the responsible party.

Accounts Receivable
- Responsible party monthly review of aged accounts receivable report: Look for and inquire as to the specifics of accounts that are entering the longer aged categories.
- Responsible party authorization for charge-offs.

Investments
- Responsible party should be provided with an investment report as a part of the monthly financial information provided by the accounting function.

Depreciable Fixed Assets
- Responsible party should be provided with a fixed assets (depreciable assets) report that agrees to the reported amounts and that includes the calculation of monthly depreciation expense.

Accounts Payable
- Responsible party should be provided with the list of aged accounts payable for review and inquiry as to the circumstances surrounding aging payables.

Sales or Service Revenue
- Responsible party should be provided with various sales reports, including trends, and a description of results that differ from expected sales results.

For the responsible party and the individual providing this information, this list may appear to be a large volume of information. However, on second glance, these should be considered basic reports that really already exist in some form as part of a decent set of accounting records. The primary difference here is that these reports are being submitted to a responsible party for *review*.

In summary, the majority of new efforts are directed at the responsible party to verify the bank reconciliation and bank account information. The remainder of the new processes generally add a review requirement on the responsible party.

By including these items in the anti-fraud program, even the smallest organization can strengthen the overall effectiveness of its program. The effectiveness is not measured by the threshold of prevention, but rather by the speed of detection.

CHAPTER EIGHT

Control Activities

General Processes

S O FAR, WE HAVE EXAMINED (1) the guiding principles of control activities design, (2) the foundational control activities that every organization should have, and (3) the necessary detection control activities for the smallest of organizations that cannot have adequate segregation of duties.

This chapter is devoted to various control activities that address a wide range of issues that can exist within transaction processes. Chapter 9 addresses control activities specific to financial statement line items.

How to document the anti-fraud program is covered in Chapter 10. The presentation in this chapter is documentation based, meaning that the information is presented as it would look in the final documented anti-fraud program.

Based on the risks identified in the fraud risk assessment, you must develop specific control activities in response.

 ## TWO OPERATIONAL QUESTIONS

As you address these risks, two all-encompassing operational questions will serve as your guide:

1. How does money go out of our organization?
2. How does money come in to our organization?

If you can answer these two questions, you have the groundwork necessary to construct specific control activities for your organization. Let's look at an example of the possible answers to the first question.

How Does Money Go Out of Our Organization?

The following list represents some possible answers to this question:

- **Checks:** We pay employees, buy inventory, and pay expenses. Our company uses checks to perform these processes.
- **Online bill payment:** We pay certain bills electronically, such as our credit card bills and our Office Depot credit account.
- **Wire transfers:** Certain larger suppliers request payment directly by wire transfer. These are usually larger dollar payments.
- **Periodic drafts:** For some of our bills, such as our monthly utility bills, we have set up an automatic draft from our bank account to accomplish payment.
- **Cash travel advances:** We provide cash to our employees for travel expense purposes.

By answering this question, it becomes clear that control activities should be directed toward shoring up these five areas.

Figure 8.1 provides an example of how to document the control activities that you have determined are necessary for check disbursements.

Figure 8.1 reflects *simple practicality.* I constantly fight the urge to document these processes with grids, flowcharts, columns for numerous purposes, and more. Although there are instances where those types of documents are necessary, they don't address simplicity at the core. In my opinion, the type of documentation exhibited in Figure 8.1 provides the current and future reader a very detailed but simple diagram of the processes in place for check disbursements.

All of these processes are tied to the bank account, so perhaps another illustration dealing with the bank reconciliation process is in order (see Figure 8.2).

Figure 8.3 details the control activities of the receipt of customer accounts receivable payments in the mail.

Observe how these illustrations work in conjunction with the fraud risk assessment outlined in Chapter 5. The fraud risk assessment framework that was completed in Chapter 5 is reproduced in Figure 8.4 for reference.

SCOTCO, Inc. **Anti-Fraud Program** **Documentation of Control Activities** **Dated: September 16, 20xx**	
Control Activities	
Disbursements with Paper Checks	
1	The authorized check signers are as follows: Jeff Chapman, Stephan Smith
2	Checks of less than $5,000 only require one signature.
3	Checks equal to or exceeding $5,000 must have the signatures of both of the authorized check signers
4	Invoices, statements, and/or payment requests are distributed from the incoming mail to the appropriate responsible department head (responsible party).
5	The responsible party compares the invoice to the purchase order and receiving slip to determine agreement.
6	The responsible party then approves the invoice for payment by initialing the invoice as approved.
7	Approved invoices are forwarded to the accounts payable department for general ledger account coding and preparation of the check.
8	The check can only be prepared if there is an approved set of supporting documentation (invoice, monthly statement, payment requests, Expense Report Form, Supplemental Business Meal and Entertainment Charges Documentation Form).
9	The checks, with the supporting documentation attached, are forwarded to the authorized check signer for signature.

10	The authorized check signer must review the check and supporting documentation for each of the following:
	    Check amount agrees to the supporting documentation
	    Supporting documentation reflects that the disbursement is for a valid business
	    purpose

11	Once satisfied, the authorized check signer initials the documentation and signs the check.
12	The authorized check signer forwards the documentation to the accounting department.
13	The accounting department makes a copy of the check, and then places the check in an envelope and into the outgoing mail basket.
14	The accounting department files the check copy and the supporting documentation together in the alphabetical invoice filing system.
15	As a part of the formal monitoring program, compliance with the review of the supporting documentation set before checks are signed will be audited periodically to determine the level of adherence to that control activity.

FIGURE 8.1   Disbursement with Paper Checks

SCOTCO, Inc.
Anti-Fraud Program
Documentation of Control Activities
Dated: September 16, 20xx

	Control Activities
Bank Reconciliations	
1	The senior accountant is responsible for performing the bank reconciliations on a monthly basis.
2	The senior accountant is not to have signature authority on the bank accounts.
3	The bank reconciliations must be completed by the third day of the month and submitted to the accounting supervisor upon completion.
4	The accounting supervisor shall review the bank reconciliations for accuracy and for follow-up issues for uncleared deposits in transit and outstanding checks as necessary.
5	Once satisfied, the accounting supervisor will initial the reconciliation as approved and file in the related company file.

FIGURE 8.2 Bank Reconciliations

SCOTCO, Inc.
Anti-Fraud Program
Documentation of Control Activities
Dated: September 16, 20xx

	Control Activities
	Customer Accounts Receivable Collections through the Mail
1	Incoming mail will be opened by one individual. The individual responsible for opening the mail will rotate weekly and includes the following positions: receptionist, accounting clerk 1, accounting clerk 2.
2	An "incoming mail receipts log" that provides the total of customer payments will be prepared by the individual opening the mail and then forwarded to the cashier, along with the daily collections.
3	The cashier will complete the "daily cash sheet" noting customer name, account number, and amount paid.
4	The cashier will compare the total of the "incoming mail receipts log" to the total per the daily cash sheet and initial as in agreement.
5	The cashier will then prepare the deposit slip from the information noted on the "daily cash sheet."
6	The daily cash sheet will be forwarded to the accounts receivable clerk (accounting clerk 2).
7	The bank bag with the checks and deposit slip will be forwarded to accounting clerk 1, who will take the deposit to the bank and obtain the validated deposit slip.
8	Accounting clerk 2 will post the payments to the individual customer accounts receivable accounts and run a "daily batch summary" of accounts receivable postings.
9	Accounting clerk 1 will bring the validated deposit slip from the bank and forward to accounting clerk 2.
10	Accounting clerk 2 will compare the "daily batch summary" of accounts receivable postings to the amount per the validated deposit slip and initial as in agreement.
11	Accounting clerk 2 will file the incoming mail log, the daily cash sheet, the daily batch summary of accounts receivable postings, and the deposit slip in the daily work file for that day.

FIGURE 8.3 Customer Accounts Receivable Collections through the Mail

Identified Fraud Risks and Schemes	Likelihood	Financial Significance	Risk Ref. No.
Misappropriation of Assets			
Bank reconciliations are performed by a position that has the ability to collect payments and post to accounts receivable, as well as the ability to post general journal entries to the ledger. This is a segregation of duties problem that could result in:			
1. Posting false deposits into the bank account to reduce employee accounts receivable balances.	With all of this control, it is very likely that numerous types of fraud could occur in this area.	Unlimited. This is the entry and exit point of all of the company funds.	1
The travel and business expense reimbursement system in place is okay, but management admits that not all of the documentation is reviewed before signing the checks. This could result in:			
1. Employees claiming reimbursement for false or fictitious items.	With the validation process not being adhered to very well, the likelihood of a false reimbursement request is high.	This seems like an opportunity for a quick take, not necessarily in large dollar amounts. Anything very large is going to show up in our expense accounts fairly quickly.	2

FIGURE 8.4 Fraud Risk Assessment Framework

Two identified fraud risks were noted in this illustration. The first dealt with the fact that the individual who performs bank reconciliations can also collect and post customer accounts receivable. Based on the control activities designed as reflected in Figures 8.2 and 8.3, this fraud risk has been addressed. No longer can the individual who performs the bank reconciliations perform these other procedures.

The second identified risk addressed the fact that the individual responsible for signing checks was not always validating the supporting documentation. The last control activity noted in Figure 8.2 provides that this function will be audited. This audit provides accountability on the part of the authorized check signer.

Please understand that there would be no possible way to address every single internal control issue that may occur within an organization. The information that follows represents those control issues most commonly noted in my fraud investigations, along with those that seem to be of a recurring nature. The information is presented as categorized by the control activity area, the condition, and the resulting fraud risk. The control activities that can address these risks are then provided.

Numerous areas are interrelated in some manner. For example, the control activities that focus on proper disbursements for the cash in bank area also cover the control activities applicable to expenses and/or fixed asset purchases. The control activities that focus on proper recording of receipts for the cash in bank area also cover control activities related to accounts receivable and to sales (revenue).

Because of these interrelated components, the remainder of this chapter presents the control activities over what I will refer to as *processes*. An example of a process is that of preparing and posting journal entries. Compare this category to control activities for specific financial statement line items such as inventory. The control activities for specific financial statement line items are presented in Chapter 9.

 ## COMMON CONTROL ACTIVITIES

The following information includes issues that should be considered when designing control activities for the most common processes.

Control Area: Disbursement Process

Condition: Review and approval of supporting documentation for disbursements is either not performed or not performed properly.

Fraud risk: Ability to perform fraudulent disbursements. Remember Larry the chief financial officer? His $1.3 million fraud was made possible because the employee responsible for signing checks did not take the time to review and validate the receipts that were stapled to his expense report form. Other case presentations reflect the same lack of adherence to existing control activities.

Control Activities

- All checks and electronic payment requests will include all supporting documentation when provided to the authorized check signer.
- The authorized check signer will determine that the check amount agrees to the supporting documentation.
- Checks in amounts exceeding $25,000 will require the signature of two authorized check signers.
- The authorized check signer will determine from a review of the supporting documentation that the disbursement is for a valid business purpose before signing the check.
- The authorized check signer will initial the supporting documentation as final approval once satisfied as to the accuracy and validity of the disbursement.
- Periodic audits for compliance with these processes will be performed by the responsible party.

Control Area: Receipt Process

Condition: The employee who collects accounts receivable payments also posts payments to individual customers' accounts and prepares and takes the deposit slip to the bank.

Fraud risk: Accounts receivable lapping, a skimming scheme (money is taken from the organization before it is recorded). Lapping is one of the most common fraud schemes I encounter in my investigation practice. In a lapping scheme, one customer's account is credited as paid, but the funds for this payment are taken from another customer's account. Here is how a lapping scheme works:

Isaac pays his monthly balance due to the organization (his account receivable). Danielle, the cashier, pockets Isaac's payment. When Isaac receives his statement from the organization next month and notices that last month's payment isn't reflected, he is going to call and complain.

No need to worry, though, because Danielle has it covered. You see, two days after the theft of Isaac's payment, Rett paid his bill. Instead of posting the payment to Rett's account, Danielle posted it to Isaac's account. Now Isaac's account is good, but Rett's isn't. Rett is going to be fine, though, because Marlee made a payment the day after Rett, and Danielle made Rett's account good with Marlee's payment.

If I were Danielle, I would get tired very quickly. However, I have seen accounts receivable lapping schemes continue for a long time. In fact, the scheme can continue until detection (most commonly resulting from Danielle being required to take vacation), restitution, or she records a general journal entry to conceal the theft.

Control Activities
- The cashier will complete the daily cash receipts sheet and prepare the deposit slip.
- The daily cash sheet will then be forwarded to the accounts receivable accounting clerk, who will post the payments to the individual customer accounts and run a daily batch summary of accounts receivable postings.
- The bank bag with the money and the deposit slip will be forwarded by the cashier to a second accounting clerk.
- The second accounting clerk will take the deposit to the bank and obtain the validated deposit slip.
- Upon return from the bank, the second accounting clerk will forward the validated deposit slip to the accounts receivable clerk, who will compare and agree the validated deposit slip to the total of the daily batch summary of accounts receivable postings and initial as in agreement.
- The accounts receivable accounting clerk will file the daily cash sheet, the daily batch summary, and the deposit slip together in the daily work file.

Control Area: Charge-Offs of Accounts, Notes, and/or Loans Receivable

Condition: There is no required approval for charge-offs of accounts, notes, or loans receivable.

Fraud risk: Concealment of fictitious or delinquent accounts. Removing a fictitious or delinquent account is very easy in an environment where no approval is required for the charge-off. Depending on the size and structure of the organization, the approval authority is represented by the board of directors, the owner, or upper management. Regardless, there should be no circumstance where an account can simply be charged off without any type of approval authority.

Let's consider the circumstance where an employee of the company has a friend or family member (or, for that matter, themselves) with an account receivable balance with the company. Let's also consider that this account receivable is for valid purchases from the company or possibly a loan from the company (as in the case of the company being a financial institution). If this were a loan from a financial institution, it could possibly be a fictitious loan disbursed by the employee in our example.

Whatever the nature of the outstanding balance, the employee desires that the balance not really be paid. So charge it off. A simple journal entry to credit the balance receivable and debit bad debt expense (or even some other expense account to hide it in) accomplishes the task. Does this really happen? Absolutely. I have encountered this circumstance repeatedly. It happens so much because it is simple, and small business owners don't want to believe that an employee will do this to them.

Control activities established in the proper manner can serve to reduce the probabilities of this type of fraud.

Control Activities

- Board of directors approval is required for charge-offs.
- Prior to the monthly board meetings, management will meet with the collections department to discuss the status of delinquent accounts and determine which accounts should be submitted for charge-off approval.
- The collections department will prepare a written charge-off report complete with account number, name, and account balance for submission to the board for approval.

Author's note: I previously used the phrase "control activities established in the proper manner" in introducing this specific set of control activities. That language was used for this specific control. I consider it absolutely necessary that the account number *and* name be included on the charge-off report that is submitted for approval. I have experienced situations where management and/or the board of directors want to include only the account number and amount when reviewing aged receivables reports or charge-off reports. Their reason is that they want to avoid the appearance of favoritism in situations where they are friends with the customer on the list. They perceive that knowing who the person is could unfairly color their opinion, in either direction, toward how they will direct management to deal with this account. This relatively noble position results in a significant reduction in the effectiveness of this specific control. If the name is required, then an employee's or family member's name should raise red flags. In addition, the perception of detection increases exponentially if employees who are considering committing the fraud know that their name must be included in the report. This one requirement almost eliminates this type of fraud.

- After discussion in the board of directors' meeting, approval will be given for the charge-off accounts.
- Management will forward the approved charge-off report to the accounting department for preparation and posting of the charge-off journal entry.
- Prior to the subsequent month's board of directors meeting, management will review this charge-off report to the general ledger activity where the charge-offs were recorded and initialed as in agreement.
- Any differences between the accounts and amounts approved and the amounts and accounts recorded will be immediately investigated and resolved.

Author's note: Once again, the proper operation of this control is contingent upon a validation, or monitoring function, as is evidenced by the comparison of approved charge-offs to actual charge-offs.

Control Area: Inventory Write-Offs Other Than the Physical Count Adjustment

Condition: No approval is required for inventory write-offs resulting from issues other than the physical count adjustment.
Fraud risk: Concealment of theft of inventory. With the establishment of the physical inventory count and adjustment procedures previously presented, concealment of theft of inventory is made more difficult. However, common entries are made to inventory accounts other than the physical count adjustment. It is a sound business practice to periodically review inventory on hand for obsolescence, spoilage, and/or shrinkage. Adjustments (journal entries) for these scenarios are necessary and should be subject to the same type of controls as the physical adjustment controls.

Control Activities
- The determination of inventory obsolescence shall be performed on a quarterly basis.

- The warehouseman, along with accounting clerk 1, should review inventory on hand for items that are old, damaged, or otherwise not acceptable for sale or use.
- Accounting clerk 1 shall prepare an inventory obsolescence report that provides the item number, description, and number of items that are considered obsolete.
- The warehouseman and accounting clerk 1 should both initial this report as complete and forward to accounting clerk 2 for the purpose of performing the cost times quantity extension calculations resulting in the amount to write off, the inventory write-off valuation report.
- The inventory write-off valuation report should then be submitted to the board of directors for approval.
- The approved inventory write-off valuation report should then be forwarded to the accounting department for preparation and posting of the write-off journal entry.

Control Area: Payroll Processing

Condition: There are no control activities established surrounding the payment of company payroll.

Fraud risk: Unauthorized disbursements concealed through the payroll process. There are numerous schemes involved in payroll fraud, ranging from ghost employees (issuing paychecks to nonexistent individuals or to individuals who do not work for the company), to falsified wage schemes (alteration of time worked), to commission schemes (improper calculations of commissions due). A small business payroll may be paid with a check or through direct deposit to the employee's bank. To reduce the probabilities of payroll fraud in a small business, a few common, well-placed control activities can be quite effective. Consider the following four components to the payroll process:

1. The employee must be created (entered into the system).
2. Time worked must be tracked (time sheets, time cards).
3. Employees must be paid (calculated hourly or salary based).
4. Payroll must be recorded.

In considering item 1, control activities should focus on the hiring process and entry of the employee into the payroll processing system. Maintaining an employee file with certain required background and reference checks documentation and personal identifying information is an absolute requirement. Photo identification, driver's license, Social Security card, résumé, authorization for rate of pay, and the like should be required and maintained in the employee personnel file.

Whether you use time sheets, time cards, or an electronic form for tracking hours worked is the focus of item 2. Item 1 provides the rate of pay, and item 2 provides the time to which the rate must be applied to perform the calculation necessary in item 3, paying the employees.

In item 3, the employee must be paid. The calculations are performed, whether hourly or salary based. The actual payment of the payroll is then accomplished in a number of ways, such as check disbursement or direct deposit in the employee's personal bank account. Item 3 addresses the issues of how much and how the employee is to be paid.

Finally, item 4 addresses the issue of how the payroll will be recorded in the accounting records.

The following basic control activities provide certain breaks in the process for segregation of duties purposes. The control activities also provide certain review processes built into the processing system that add a certain amount of control for those organizations that cannot accomplish segregation of duties due to staff size. Like certain other control areas, performing some type of audit or monitoring procedures may be necessary to lessen the time between when fraud begins and when it is detected.

Control Activities

- A criminal background check and reference checking will be a part of the hiring process.
- A personnel file will be maintained for each employee, which may include:
    Background checks
    Reference checks
    Résumé
    Identifying information (driver's license, Social Security card)
    Authorization for salary or rate of pay
- Information regarding name, address, Social Security number, and authorized rate of pay will be entered into the payroll processing system by accounting clerk 1.
- Addresses, Social Security numbers, and driver's license numbers for new employees will be cross-referenced with existing employees for purposes of identifying potential ghost employees.
- For hourly employees, time sheets will be prepared by the employee for hours worked and submitted to their supervisor for review and approval.

- Once approved, time sheets will be forwarded to accounting clerk 2 for entry of hours worked into the payroll processing system.
- Accounting clerk 2 will also review commission calculation forms for accuracy.
- Once the hours and commissions payable are entered into the payroll processing system, an initial payroll register for the period will be produced and forwarded to accounting clerk 1.
- Accounting clerk 1 will review the list of employees paid against a list of company employees and initial as to agreement.
- Accounting clerk 1 will review the initial payroll register for reasonableness of the pay amounts, looking for input errors that may have occurred.
- Accounting clerk 1 will initial the register and return it to accounting clerk 2.
- Accounting clerk 2, only on presentation of an approved payroll register from accounting clerk 1, will finalize the payroll register, which results in the preparation of the paychecks or direct deposit file.
- For paper checks, the control activities surrounding the paper check disbursement process will apply.
- For direct deposit, the direct deposit file will be forwarded to the authorized check signer, and the control activities surrounding the electronic disbursement process will apply.
- For paper checks, the paychecks will be distributed to the employees by the accounting supervisor, who has no part in the process of the production of paychecks.
- If not directly interfaced, accounting clerk 2 will post the payroll register information to the general ledger.
- The accounting supervisor will review the posting of the payroll against the payroll register information and initial as to agreement.

Control Area: Contract Procurement and Competitive Bid Process

Condition: The procurement processes do not include procedures for awarding contracts or any delineation for large item purchases.

Fraud risk: Conflicts of interest, procurement corruption. Two situations are covered in this section:

1. Large-dollar-item purchase controls
2. Awarding of contracts

Sometimes these are interrelated; sometimes they are not. They will be presented here as interrelated. The issues in this area address many potential frauds, such as preferential treatment of a supplier, the risk of kickbacks, the disbursement of a large amount of company funds at one time, and possibly conflicts of interest in the sales and disbursements processes. Let's see how these can apply with an example.

Brock Industries needs to purchase a specialized mobile modular building that houses circuit electronics out in the field, a large-dollar item. Tanner, the purchasing agent for the company, has a brother-in-law, James, who just happens to own a company that sells these items. Being the opportunist that he is, Tanner swings a deal with James to sell the company this item for $75,000. The actual retail price of this item averages about $65,000. In a classic kickback scheme, James agrees to split the $10,000 profit from the sale with Tanner. This works so well that Tanner and James repeat this type of fraud numerous times over five years. By the time the fraud is detected, Tanner and James have each recognized $100,000 in personal profits. Over this five-year period, the company has overpaid $200,000 for these items.

This type of fraud is also common because of the absence of control activities related to large-dollar purchasing. What if Brock Industries had a control activity requiring items costing over $25,000 to be subject to approval by two supervisors or by the board of directors? Now Tanner and James have an increased perception of detection.

But Tanner and James also know that they can possibly split this item into portions that are billed as four separate items in amounts of about $19,000 each. But what if Brock Industries had competitive bid requirements for amounts anticipated to exceed $25,000? Now, not only do Tanner and James perceive a better chance of being detected but also the fraud itself is much more difficult to perpetrate.

Whether it is a large-dollar item or a construction contract type of issue, the control activities referenced can go a long way toward deterring this type of fraud.

Control Activities

- On an annual basis, all employees will complete the conflicts of interest form detailing the nature of any business relationships or conflicts, familial or ownership or both, they could potentially have with suppliers and service providers for Brock Industries.
- Disbursements that are anticipated to exceed $25,000 must be approved by the board of directors.

- Contracts or disbursements anticipated to exceed $25,000 are subject to the competitive bidding process outlined here.
- Competitive bidding requirements for contracts or disbursements anticipated to exceed $25,000 include the following:

    Bid requirements will be determined by the applicable department head.

    The bid requirements will be advertised upon approval of management.

    A minimum of three sealed bids will be required.

    Sealed bids will be opened after the bid submission deadline and evaluated according to various criteria, such as cost, compliance with the bid requirements, and bondability.

    The accepted bid contract or invoice will be signed by management after ratification by the board of directors.
- Contracts awarded or disbursements made in excess of $25,000 will be reviewed by the board audit committee on an annual basis for compliance with these control activities.

Author's note: One of the standard investigative procedures I use is to obtain a record of disbursements to data-mine for trends that reflect a large number of disbursements just under the established threshold amounts per the company policy. Detection of transactions structured to fall below these thresholds is most often indicative that fraud has occurred.

Control Area: Journal Entries

Condition: Journal entries can be posted for most issues that occur in a set of financial statements with no approval.

Fraud risk: Everything! That is not an overstatement. Virtually any type of fraud can be concealed by posting a simple journal entry. The majority of frauds that I investigate have been successfully concealed by a journal entry. Interestingly enough, the majority of small businesses that I deal with have absolutely no controls in this area. Not limited or weak controls. No controls. If someone were to ask me what the magic bean of fraud prevention is, I would respond first with increasing the perception of detection. My second response would be journal entries. You have to establish controls surrounding the journal entry process. When the term *journal entries* is used in this section, it refers to nonstandard journal entries as compared to fixed journal entries. Numerous fixed journal entries are posted to the accounting records on a monthly basis. Common examples of fixed journal entries are depreciation expense entries, prepaid expense amortization entries, and some regular accrual journal entries.

So what can happen? Well, Larry the chief financial officer was able to conceal his large-dollar fraud by posting journal entries to reduce the travel expense account and spread the dollars to other accounts within the financial statements. Had he not done this, the actual balance in travel expenses would have exceeded the annual budget for travel expenses by the second month of the fiscal year.

Accounts receivable lapping schemes, discussed earlier, are difficult and time-consuming for the perpetrator to keep up with. Can you imagine going to work every day realizing that you had to keep track of what you stole the day before, the day before that, and continuing backward in time? Personally, I would wear out. But with a simple clearing journal entry to post the proper credits to the customer accounts with an offset to just about anywhere, the accounts receivable account balance is good, the customer accounts are good, and I can start fresh, committing the same fraud again.

CASE: THE CELL PHONE REIMBURSEMENT

DeAnn was the executive director of a small local nonprofit organization. As with many organizations, DeAnn was provided a company cell phone for business use. The cell phone was to be with her all the time, and thus it was accepted that it would result in some personal use. To recognize this fact, the board of directors of the company adopted a policy that DeAnn would reimburse the company monthly for exactly half of the cell phone bill. So she did; she recorded a journal entry each month to reflect as a bank deposit, with the offset as a posting to reduce the cell phone expense account.

DeAnn reimbursed her company in this manner for 13 months before the fraud was detected from the review of one of the current bank reconciliations. This review revealed 13 uncleared deposits in transit, beginning with the current month and going backward in time for 12 previous months. The reviewer knew that an uncleared deposit in transit on a bank reconciliation is a major indicator of fraud. A check could remain outstanding for several months for any number of reasons, but a deposit in transit should absolutely clear within the next two business days at least. DeAnn didn't get rich off this scheme. In fact, for the $900 she gained personally over 13 months, her career ended. In considering the design of control activities surrounding the journal entry process, one unfortunate fact should be understood. Often, the innocent employee posting the journal entry is not paying much attention to what is being posted. Employees are just doing their jobs. It's not a career; it's a job. I don't desire to appear critical, but I do desire to be honest. This is a fact that I witness almost daily.

However, the special aspect applicable to journal entries is that they are commonly and frequently used to *conceal* fraud but are used just as much to *commit* fraud. Financial statement fraud is so easily committed by the journal entry, the stroke of a pen, so to speak.

Accordingly, with a few well-thought-out control activities in place, the primary tool used to *conceal* and *commit* fraud is virtually taken away from the perpetrator.

Control Activities

- Every nonstandard journal entry requires the completion of a journal entry voucher.
- Documentation that supports the nature, reason, and amount of the journal entry should be attached to the journal entry voucher.
- Journal entry vouchers shall be forwarded to the accounting supervisor for review and approval as evidenced by the initials.
- Journal entry vouchers requested by the accounting supervisor shall be forwarded to and approved by management.
- Once approved, the journal entry vouchers shall be forwarded to accounting clerk 1 or accounting clerk 2 for posting to the general ledger.
- Journal entries will not be posted to the general ledger without the approved documentation attached to the approved journal entry voucher.
- The accounting clerk who posted the journal entry to the general ledger shall initial the approved journal entry voucher.
- Journal entry vouchers and the supporting documentation will be filed numerically in the accounting department files.
- Auditing for compliance with these control activities will be performed periodically.

Control Area: New Vendor Establishment

Condition: No procedures exist for the establishment of new vendors.
Fraud risk: Shell company disbursement fraud. The example in Chapter 6 outlines the methods used by fraud perpetrators to cause disbursements to be made to fictitious companies or outside companies owned by the perpetrator. These are known as shell companies. Proper new vendor establishment procedures

that include validation procedures can significantly reduce opportunities for fraud in this area.

Control Activities

- A master vendor file will be maintained and updated on a periodic basis.
- The new vendor establishment form will be initiated within the accounts payable department for all potential new vendors.
- Information to be obtained for the form will be requested from the potential new vendor and completed by accounts payable clerk 1.
- Accounts payable clerk 1 will forward the new vendor establishment form to accounts payable clerk 2.
- Accounts payable clerk 2 is responsible for validating the information on the new vendor establishment form. Validation procedures will include:
  Test phone calls to the phone numbers provided
  Test e-mail message to the e-mail address provided
  Web-based search engine inquiries
  State tax base searches
  Online mapping or Google Earth searches of addresses provided
- Accounts payable clerk 2 will forward the completed and validated new vendor establishment form to management for approval.
- The approved and completed new vendor establishment form, along with any other documentation obtained from the vendor (e.g., articles of incorporation), will be added to the master vendor file.
- As a part of the formal monitoring program, compliance with the process detailed here will be audited annually.

Other Control Activity Considerations

Control activities are designed to reduce the probabilities of determined fraud risks becoming reality. The control activities presented focus on certain areas identified as processes.

In identifying financial statement areas, all balance sheets include assets, liabilities, and equity. All income statements include revenue (sales) and expenses. Process areas can include areas such as receipts, disbursements, shipping, receiving, and cash register sales. The purpose in mentioning this is that all of these areas, however identified, can interrelate in some form or fashion. Accounts receivable interrelates with sales, accounts payable interrelates with disbursements, disbursements interrelates with expenses, and so on.

The next chapter provides control activities for certain financial statement line items, as opposed to the control activities for processes presented in this chapter.

The control activities designations included in the written anti-fraud program should be tailored specifically to your organization, not to some model presentation that may or may not fit the operations, size, and level of complexity of your company.

There is no way to illustrate all control activities necessary to address all possible occurrences of fraud. This information is presented to illustrate how to think, how to design, and how to document the control activities specific to the fraud risks relevant to your organization.

CHAPTER NINE

Control Activities

Specific Control Areas

C ONTROL ACTIVITIES FOR GENERAL PROCESSES were presented in Chapter 8. This chapter is devoted to the various control activities associated with specific line items on the financial statement, such as inventory or investments. It should be understood that all control activities will be a part of the control activities section of the final documented anti-fraud program as presented in Chapter 13.

The presentation in this chapter is formatted in the same manner as those control activities presented in Chapter 8. The introductory information included in that chapter applies equally to the control activities presented here.

FINANCIAL STATEMENT LINE ITEM CONTROL ACTIVITIES

Control Area: Cash in Bank

Condition: The individual responsible for performing bank reconciliations can also sign checks and perform electronic payments.

Fraud risk: Ability to perform and conceal fraudulent disbursements. An example is an employee's ability to disburse funds for personal purposes, such as a personal mortgage payment or any of a multitude of other personal expenses. In this circumstance, the employee has the custody of the asset, can authorize transactions related to this asset, and has the ability to record transactions related to this asset. Therefore, the employee can conceal disbursement fraud for an extended period of time.

Control Activities

- Employees responsible for performing bank reconciliations are prohibited from signing checks or performing other electronic means of disbursement.
- Bank reconciliations, when complete, should be forwarded to the accounting supervisor for review and approval.

Control Area: Accounts Receivable Allowance for Uncollectible Accounts

Condition: No reasonable, methodical approach exists for determining the adequacy of the balance in the allowance for uncollectible accounts.

Fraud risk: Misstatement of the financial statements. One of the simplest ways to make the financial statements appear better than reality is through misstatement of the allowance account. This is accomplished by having no methodology in place to determine the proper necessary balance. Numerous methods can be used to provide this estimate. By way of example, one reasonable, methodical approach is based on history, also referred to as the experience method. Under this method, an aged accounts receivable report should be produced at the end of each month and then, based on past experience, percentages of historical loss that have occurred in each category can be applied to these current categorical balances. When summed, the total represents the necessary balance in the allowance for uncollectible accounts.

Control Activities

- The calculation of the desired balance in the allowance for uncollectible accounts will be performed at the end of each month by the accounting supervisor prior to preparation of the month-end closing journal entries.
- The journal entry to adjust the allowance account will be prepared and submitted for approval by management.
- Once approved, the journal entry will be posted by accounting clerk 1.

Control Area: Investments

Condition: There are no control activities associated with investment purchases and sales.

Fraud risk: Unauthorized fraudulent investment purchases and sales. The policies of an organization should include an investment policy that outlines the types of authorized investments in which it will invest excess funds. The policy addresses issues specific to the organization, such as investment thresholds and risk tolerance. Compliance with these investment objectives is necessary, and procedures should be in place to audit for policy compliance. However, that is not an issue of fraud prevention. The fraud risk enters the picture when employees purchase and sell investments in their own names with company funds. I have investigated several instances where the investment manager employee was doing quite well on these types of investments. Because he was the investment manager and purchasing agent, his name was associated with various investments, the income of which was deposited directly into his personal bank account.

Control Activities

- Investments will be purchased in the name of the company only.
- Investment sales and purchases will occur only on approval of the investment committee.
- CUSIP confirmation slips for purchases and sales will be retained by the accounting department.
- The accounting supervisor will prepare a month-end investment report and submit to management and/or the board of directors for monthly review.
- Semiannual audits of the listed investments against the safekeeping information and CUSIP confirmation information will be performed by the investment committee or audit committee of the board of directors.

Control Area: Inventory

Condition: There are no physical controls over the inventory warehouse and no periodic inventory counts performed.

Fraud risk: Physical theft of inventory. Depending on the type and industry of the organization, the term *inventory* can refer to a supply type of inventory, such as construction materials, or to merchandise inventory, represented by the retail items the organization sells. Regardless, the concepts surrounding inventory control are equally necessary. The number of occurrences of actual inventory theft that I have encountered is staggering. The ability to control this area is relatively simple.

Control Activities
- Access to inventory locations will be locked after hours and under the control of the custodian of the warehouse (warehouseman during business hours).
- Inventory will be issued from the warehouse only upon presentation of a properly completed and authorized inventory issue request form.
- Inventory returns require an inventory return slip that provides the item number, condition, and original issue value.
- At the end of each quarter, the accounting department will produce a perpetual inventory report count sheet that provides the item number and quantity on hand in the accounting records.
- Accounting clerk 2 will take this perpetual inventory count sheet and, together with the warehouseman, perform a physical count of the inventory on hand, noting the actual count of items on hand next to the perpetual record number of items on hand.
- Accounting clerk 2 and a senior warehouseman will both initial the count as complete.
- Accounting clerk 2 will forward the count sheet to accounting clerk 1, who will input the count numbers into the perpetual inventory count system to produce an inventory variance report.
- Accounting clerk 2 and the warehouseman will recount those items that represent a significant variance; explanations will be provided for these inventory differences.
- Once the counts are double-verified, accounting clerk 1 will run the final inventory variance report and prepare the necessary adjusting journal entry to record the inventory difference (overage or shortage).
- The system will automatically update the perpetual inventory system with the new final counts.

●   ●   ●

Condition: There are no physical controls over the inventory warehouse or capitalized equipment owned by the organization.

Fraud risk: Abuse of use of inventory items. Inventory theft is a common type of fraud, and abuse of use of inventory or fixed-asset items could be considered just as common. Specifically, abuse of use occurs when employees use an inventory or fixed-assets item for personal purposes.

Consider the following example: The organization owns a high-dollar tractor-shredder that is useful for cutting large lots or fields for construction projects. Tim the salesman has a personal home project this weekend that would go so much better if he used that tractor-shredder. Tim loads the tractor-shredder onto the company trailer, pulled by the company truck, and completes his weekend project. He then takes it all back to the company yard late on Sunday afternoon. If this same situation is repeated by various other employees frequently, the life of this tractor-shredder as used for company purposes will be significantly shortened. This is what I refer to as abuse of use. This situation may not necessarily always indicate a major problem, but it quite often does. The issue at hand is that the company has no way to control what is happening to the tractor-shredder. The simple control activities of disclosure and authorization provide the company the ability to control what happens to the tractor-shredder. Of course, management must then decide what type of liability risk is associated with the planned use, considering issues such as the experience level of the user and the area where the equipment will be used.

Control Activities
- Personal use of company fixed assets or inventory will be determined by management on a case-by-case basis.
- The proper request for personal use form will be completed by the requesting employee and submitted to management.
- Management will either approve or deny the request, based on factors such as level of planned personal use, length of time needed for personal use, and upcoming planned business use of the asset.
- If approved, the asset will be checked out with a completed checkout slip prepared by the warehouseman and will be inspected by the warehouseman upon return to the warehouse. A return slip will be prepared by the warehouseman and signed by the employee returning the equipment.

• • •

These control activities over specific financial statement line items represent those areas where I encounter the most problems. The areas for which each company will design specific control activities is a function of the industry, the product or service, and the level of complexity of operations.

PART THREE

Completing the Anti-Fraud Program: The Ceiling, the Roof, and Routine Maintenance

OW THAT THE WALLS ARE UP, we need to put a ceiling on the structure. As soon as the ceiling is in place, we can put the roof over the structure and be done.

In our building metaphor, the ceiling is represented by the program documentation element and the company fraud training program element. These elements are so important in providing strength and security to the design structure. Without the proper documentation of the program, we have nothing to follow, no assurance or security that the program can even last. It would resemble a house with walls, but no ceiling to connect them and tie them all together. If we do have proper program documentation but no plan to communicate the program to our workforce, there is no strength to the program. Again, if the employees know nothing about the program, it has no strength.

Finally, the structure needs a roof. A roof protects a structure from outside influences. Because of its importance to the structure, routine maintenance is necessary. We must maintain the program. The monitoring and routine maintenance element of program design provides the maintenance necessary to protect the program by keeping it current and relevant. Just as your business grows and changes, so should your program.

The chapters in this part present a methodology for properly document-ing the contents of the anti-fraud program, along with the training program necessary to educate the workforce about the program. The monitoring func-tion determines where the weaknesses, if any, are in the effectiveness of the program. Once determined, we can perform routine maintenance on these weaknesses as is evidenced by program amendments that enhance the long-term effectiveness of the program.

This part ends with a chapter that presents an example of an entire writ-ten anti-fraud program, including all of the design elements presented in the book. This example program is to be used as a reference when you design an anti-fraud program for your company.

CHAPTER TEN

The Ceiling

Documenting the Anti-Fraud Program

THE FOUNDATION IS SOLID, THE FLOOR IS DOWN, and the walls are up. It's time to put a ceiling on the structure. That ceiling represents the information and communication elements of the anti-fraud program. The information aspect of the anti-fraud program addresses how to document the program sufficiently to enable employees, present and future, to properly function in their assigned roles. Chapter 11 presents the communication element.

 INFORMATION

Remember, the employee serving in a position today may not be the same person in that position tomorrow. The cause could be a death, a retirement, a resignation, or a termination, but the effect is the same.

Everyone has probably played the telephone party game. All of the participants form a circle, and the first person creates a statement and whispers it into the ear of the person to the left. That person turns to the left and whispers the statement that was heard. The last person in the circle to hear the statement tells it out loud to everyone in the room. Seldom, if ever, does the final statement resemble the first statement. Such is the case with an unwritten, undocumented anti-fraud program.

Training new employees often omits important aspects of control activities that would be good for them to know. We forget, we get lax, and we tend to remember about half of the specific control activities applicable to our job functions. This gives rise to preferential treatment for some control activities and to completely ignoring others. In this environment, the unwritten, undocumented control activities seldom resemble their original structure and intent.

DOCUMENTATION—KEEPING IT SIMPLE

There has been so much work involved in getting to this point in the development of your anti-fraud program. How this program is documented is crucial to honoring this amount of work. Throughout the preceding chapters, we have provided documentation examples, including policies and forms to use in putting the anti-fraud program together. So with all of this information in existence, how do we put it all together into an understandable, easy-to-follow format?

THE ELEMENTS OF HIGH-QUALITY DOCUMENTATION

As I introduce this documentation methodology, you will notice the absence of checklists, flowcharts, conversation bubbles, and the like. In keeping with our goal of *simple practicality*, this documentation format is straightforward and designed to be somewhat conversational in its approach.

Documentation Format

The documentation format is narrative in design. Throughout the narrative presentation, the following specific format is used:

Title of Document: "Anti-Fraud Program"

Title of Area Addressed
- ▪ **Introduction:** This section will state clearly that the {governing body, owner} takes the issue of fraud seriously and will not tolerate fraud of any kind. The definition of internal fraud and the types of fraud are presented as an introduction to the nature of the subject matter. This introduction sets the proper tone at the top necessary for the establishment of a proper anti-fraud environment.
- ▪ **Policies of protection:** The existence of these policies is specifically referenced in this section to further enhance the importance placed on the anti-fraud environment.

- **Fraud risk assessment:** The reasons for a fraud risk assessment are reiterated in this section, along with specific responsibilities and procedural steps for how to perform the risk assessment.
- **Control activities:** This area should address the specifics as to how the control activities are to be developed and reference where the control activities are located. It is important to note that this section also includes specific consequences for the lack of adherence to control activities. As such, this anti-fraud program, much like a policy, can and does include a legal basis for actions taken against an employee.

  This one issue is extremely important when considering the anti-fraud program as a whole. Compare it to a policy; a policy includes provisions that must be followed, the failure of which subjects an employee to the consequences of this failure. There would be no instance where an employee would not be provided the company policies. After all, how can an employee be accountable to something if he or she doesn't know it exists? Don't allow your anti-fraud program to be documented, only to sit on a shelf for no one to see.

  With these types of consequences written into the anti-fraud program, it would be considered negligent on the part of the governing body or owner to not communicate the program with the same level of importance as a policy. In fact, the anti-fraud program should be considered on a level above the policies level.

- **Information: Program documentation:** As the subject of this chapter, this section will provide the reasons for documenting the anti-fraud program and outline how the documentation will be accomplished.
- **Communication: The company fraud training program:** As discussed and illustrated in Chapters 11 and 13, this section should provide the framework for how the anti-fraud program is communicated to the workforce. This section will also include the requirements of conducting a continuous fraud awareness training program for the company.
- **Monitoring and routine maintenance:** As discussed and illustrated in Chapters 12 and 13, this section will define the various aspects of monitoring, which we will also refer to as compliance auditing throughout the remainder of this book. This section will include the procedural steps for how to determine and implement revisions to the program to maintain it on a current basis.

Below each title area will be various subcategories that apply to that area.

The following represents an example of documentation for areas covered thus far in this book.

MED ENTERPRISES, INC.

Company Anti-Fraud Program

Introduction

The board of directors of MED Enterprises, Inc. (the "Company") has established this program to address the risk of occurrences of internal fraud. *Internal fraud* is defined as fraud perpetrated against the Company by our own employees. The purpose also includes the establishment of an environment that promotes and recognizes honesty and integrity in the workforce and a safe and pleasant working atmosphere.

Internal fraud includes three types of fraud: misappropriation, corruption, and financial statement fraud, illustrated as follows:

Misappropriation: This is defined as the taking of company assets, whether cash, inventory, or other fixed assets. This is the most common type of fraud.

Corruption: This type of fraud is represented by collusion between at least two individuals (one employee and a nonemployee or two employees), including conflicts of interest in purchasing and sales schemes, bribery in kickbacks and bid-rigging schemes, illegal gratuities, and economic extortion.

Financial statement fraud: This fraud includes the intentional misrepresentation of the financial position or results of operations of the Company.

POLICIES OF PROTECTION

Certain policies have been established that provide protection for not only the Company but for each employee as well. On the date of employment, each employee will receive an employee manual that includes the complete text of policies established by the board of directors. As relates to fraud, the following three policies have been adopted:

Fraud Policy

We want you to know that we take the issue of internal fraud seriously. We have adopted a no tolerance position regarding fraud and desire the workforce to join us in this level of dedication to fraud prevention and detection. This policy was adopted to provide information about fraud, what to do if you suspect fraud, and our obligations to investigate suspicions of fraud. The policy also outlines the administrative actions that will be applied if you are suspected of the perpetration of internal fraud.

Fraud Reporting Policy

This policy was adopted to provide you with the opportunity to anonymously report suspicions of fraud. A healthy workforce is the result of your feeling as if you have someone to turn to in reporting suspicions. The policy outlines the process to follow in reporting any suspicions and our responsibilities to investigate these issues.

Expense Reimbursement Policy

The protection of and accountability for Company funds is of prime importance to us. We recognize that needs often arise for the use of Company funds for various purposes, such as travel and other purchasing needs. This policy was established to provide a sound accountability framework that ensures proper reporting, as well as protection for you, the employee.

FRAUD RISK ASSESSMENT

Introduction

A formal fraud risk assessment process is required by this anti-fraud program. The fraud risk assessment is to be performed biannually by the fraud risk assessment team as identified later.

The purpose of the fraud risk assessment process is to identify those areas of transaction performance and recording that are most vulnerable to fraud. Control activities to address these identified areas are developed by the control activities development team as identified in the control activities section of this program.

Fraud Risk Assessment Team

The fraud risk assessment team shall include the following staff positions:

Management (executive and middle)

Accounting supervisor

Sales manager

Human resources manager

(continued)

Billing supervisor

Customer service manager

In-house legal counsel

The risk assessment team shall conduct the biannual risk assessment meetings over a three-week time period in April of the applicable year. The team shall appoint a facilitator from among the team members for the purpose of scheduling and organizing the content of the meetings.

The fraud risk assessment shall be documented utilizing the fraud risk assessment framework included as Appendix A to this program. (Author's note: The actual Appendix A is included with the sample anti-fraud program as presented in Chapter 13.)

Once completed, the fraud risk assessment framework shall be provided to the control activities development team to serve as a guide for the performance of their responsibilities as defined.

Though the risk assessment team is only required to perform the assessment on a biannual basis, team members should be aware of operational changes that could result in additional vulnerabilities to fraud.

The facilitator of the risk assessment team shall inform executive management of any new vulnerability that may be identified in between fraud risk assessments. Executive management has the responsibility to present these new vulnerabilities to the control activities development team for inclusion in the anti-fraud program if determined necessary.

CONTROL ACTIVITIES

Introduction

Control activities are defined as those activities, controls, checks and balances, and processes that have been implemented to address the risks of internal fraud in our Company.

A control activity can be as simple as the requirement for two authorized signatures on checks over a certain dollar amount and as complex as a complete policy, such as the expense reimbursement policy.

Control Activities Development Team

The control activities development team shall include the following staff positions:

Executive management

Accounting supervisor

In-house legal counsel

Upon receipt of the fraud risk assessment framework, the team shall develop certain and specific control activities that address the identified fraud risks. Control activities shall be documented using the control activities form included as Appendix B to this program. (Author's note: The actual Appendix B is included with the sample anti-fraud program as presented in Chapter 13.)

Communication of Control Activities

The complete anti-fraud program, including specific control activities, will be issued in its entirety on June 1, utilizing the following means of communication:

Electronic distribution: Company intranet, e-mail

Print distribution: As part of this anti-fraud program

Continuous training: As directed by this program

The level of communication and training related to control activities will be conducted to ensure a thorough understanding of the requirements imposed upon all staff positions.

Compliance with Control Activities

Control activities have been developed over time with an extensive amount of effort. It is required that control activities applying to your specific position will be followed. We encourage staff to ask questions if there is a lack of understanding of any control activity. Failure to adhere to the various control activities will result in the following:

First violation: Formal reprimand and retraining if necessary

Second violation: Termination

As a part of the ongoing monitoring aspect of this program, we encourage you to submit to executive management any suggestions you may have for improving specific control activities.

Specific Control Activities

Specific control activities that have been placed into operation are included as Appendix C to this program. (Author's note: The actual Appendix C is included with the sample anti-fraud program as presented in Chapter 13.)

INFORMATION: PROGRAM DOCUMENTATION

This anti-fraud program, through the collective efforts of the governing body/owner, management, and staff, has been developed to address the risk of internal fraud. The contents of this anti-fraud program are required to be in written form. As such, this anti-fraud program documentation is intended as the complete documentation necessary to evidence the program.

The management of the Company is responsible for documenting all aspects of this program. Upon completion of the various documentation forms (fraud risk assessment framework, control activities forms), the responsible parties shall forward that information to management for assembly into this formal anti-fraud program.

The program shall then be submitted to the governing body/owner for approval. Once approved, this anti-fraud program shall be considered in effect.

The communication of and staff training for this program is addressed in the communication section of the program. However, the program is available at all times on the Company intranet and is provided to each employee in printed form and through electronic distribution via the Company e-mail system.

As you can see, these examples follow the simple title area format as presented here. An example of the documented anti-fraud program is presented in its entirety in Chapter 13.

CHAPTER ELEVEN

The Ceiling

The Company Fraud Training Program

O VER A DECADE AGO, THE AUDITING STANDARDS BOARD OF THE American Institute of Certified Public Accountants issued Statement on Auditing Standards No. 99: "Consideration of Fraud in a Financial Statement Audit." One of the new provisions of the standard for financial statement auditors is the requirement to ask employees, many employees, if they are aware of any fraud or suspicions of fraud that is occurring in their company.

As a financial statement auditor, I was encouraged by the fact that my profession recognized the importance of including this type of provision in the auditing literature. With my obvious love of fraud detection and investigation, I looked forward with great anticipation to this new method of soliciting information about potential fraud.

To say that I was unprepared for the answers I would receive is an understatement. It's a simple question that can be answered yes or no. If yes, then please expand. It didn't quite turn out to be that simple. The following is a list, not all-inclusive, of some of the answers I would get:

"No, I don't think so. We don't even have a website."
"No, our cyber-security is second to none."
"Yes, but I can't tell you what or who it is."

"Our company doesn't allow pets." (Author's note: Let that one sink in for a minute.)

and finally,

"Huh? What?"

Without even a close second, this last answer was the predominant response I received when asking the question. It became abundantly clear to me that no one knew what fraud was. Not only did they not know what fraud was, some had not even heard the word *fraud*. It also became abundantly clear to me that we had a lot of ground to cover when it came to increasing the level of fraud awareness in organizations. At the same time, we constantly received pushback from management that took the form of "don't ask them about fraud . . . it will only put ideas in their heads." Based on that type of statement alone, I immediately knew the quality of their anti-fraud environment. My response to them was that "employees steal . . . all of the time . . . whether or not we've trained them to do it."

More than 10 years later, I am sad to report that I still don't encounter many workforces that have been educated on the importance of a strong anti-fraud environment and the need for a sound anti-fraud program. This is why I consider communication one of the most important elements of a strong anti-fraud program.

THE ELEMENTS OF EFFECTIVE COMMUNICATION

I am firmly convinced that ineffective communication will be the downfall of society. We have digressed to the point of complete text message and e-mail communication. I'm guilty of telling people that the best way to get in touch with or communicate with me is through e-mail. We all have cell phones in hand, yet for most of us, the least used feature of our phone is the phone. Live communication is becoming a thing of the past. All of the paralinguistics and body language necessary to properly communicate are lost in written communication.

The communication aspect of the anti-fraud program should be designed to address what is lost in written communication. So far, you have expended a large amount of time and resources in the development of the anti-fraud program. The policies, the risk assessment, the control activities, and the documented anti-fraud program are all in place. So how is this program going to be communicated to the workforce, to those who are responsible for carrying out the directives of the program? It could be posted on the company intranet. It could be delivered electronically to all employees through the company e-mail system. A copy could be printed for each employee and left in a binder on every desk. Or it could be the basis of periodic, live anti-fraud or fraud awareness training. All of these communication methods are effective to varying degrees, but the most effective method will always be live communication as a part of continuous fraud awareness training.

Written documentation made available for reading, in the best case scenario, will result in employees knowing *how* to do what they do. Live presentations and live training will result in employees knowing *why* they do what they do.

Why Should We Teach Our Employees How to Commit Fraud?

Fraud awareness training does not teach or result in fraud *perpetration* training. This is a backward way of thinking, and we need to move past that type of attitude if we are to have an adequate training program. Think back to the days prior to January 1, 2000, when we were getting ready for Y2K. Every minute of every day and most of our company resources (money) were devoted to ensuring that the world wouldn't end on January 1, 2000. Months were spent and thousands of dollars invested with the hope that catastrophe and chaos would be averted. Here is a shocking fact. The total amount spent on Y2K preparedness equaled what our nation loses *annually* in fraud losses. The year 2000 did not bring the world to a halt as theorized. But extreme financial loss through fraud is happening in our businesses every single year. Yet, I don't see our companies spend resources anywhere close to what was spent on Y2K preparedness. We have to do more than we are doing.

The Structure of Continuous Fraud Awareness Training

When considering how to structure a training program, the first operative word to consider is *continuous*. Fraud awareness training is a process that should never end. It should be conducted at intervals that are frequent enough to ensure that awareness does not wane. Training sessions can be conducted monthly, quarterly, annually, or biannually, depending on the nature of the training as outlined here.

Just as significant as *continuous*, remember the very word *communication*. It is at this point that we remember that the primary purpose of the communication section of the anti-fraud program is to communicate to the workforce the purpose and inner workings of the program.

The third and final issue to consider is who. This word speaks to not only *who* will be involved in the training, but *who* will be conducting the training. In answer to the first *who*, it should include everyone. In answer to the second *who*, it depends.

The trainer must have confidence in the subject matter. In most cases, the training will be conducted by upper management. However, it is understood that some organizations do not have individuals who know the subject matter well enough to teach it. Even though upper management is a primary participant in the development of the program, they may not feel confident enough to educate the workforce on its various nuances. Some organizations have a staff position devoted to workforce education. In those organizations, this individual will suffice as the *who*. Some organizations will contract with outside parties to conduct the training. I have personally participated as the trainer for numerous anti-fraud program communication requirements. Additionally, I have trained employees to conduct the other periodic training required in the program. The primary issue is that the training be done by qualified individuals.

In summary, this structure emphasizes the continuous nature of providing high-quality education regarding fraud, along with the importance the governing body/owner places on prevention. With this emphasis in place, the following information provides a specific framework for the design of the communication and training program:

 ## THE COMPANY FRAUD TRAINING PROGRAM

The starting point for fraud training should be the presentation of the anti-fraud program. As dictated by the specific time requirements presented previously, the example training schedule is presented.

Anti-Fraud Program

June 1 (biannually): Distribution of the Anti-Fraud Program to the Workforce

The anti-fraud program will be distributed through the company intranet, through an electronic document attached to the company e-mail system, and through a hard-copy printout of the program to each employee.

Comments: Various distribution options exist. It is my opinion that all of these options should be selected to provide the most coverage. It should also be noted that outside parties such as vendors, contractors, and suppliers should be provided a copy of the fraud policy and fraud reporting policy as a part of being established as a new vendor.

By June 15 (biannually): Companywide Training on the Anti-Fraud Program

Within the two-week time period after the distribution of the anti-fraud program, the company will have conducted specific training on all aspects of the program to all employees.

Comments: The company will perform this companywide training either as a one- or two-day session for all employees simultaneously or will provide the training to all employees through several different partial workforce sessions over the two-week time period. Regardless, the presentation and training on the new anti-fraud program must be conducted for all employees within this two-week time period.

By July 15 (biannually): Departmental Related Specific Control Activities Training

During the four-week time period following the presentation of the new anti-fraud program, the company will conduct training regarding specific control activities related to the respective departments.

Comments: While it would be great for everyone to know everything, it is simply not reasonable to expect that in most companies. The control activities included in the anti-fraud program address all control areas of an organization. However, it would be of little value for the customer service department to be intimate with the specific control activities that apply to the accounting department. Therefore, training that is directed toward specific departments is necessary. This represents a secondary, higher level of training that is directed at specific departments and builds on the companywide training conducted earlier.

Training on an As-Needed Basis

The monitoring and routine maintenance element of the anti-fraud program, presented in the next chapter, results in a continuous fine-tuning or routine maintenance of the anti-fraud program. As dictated by this process, changes in control activities and other provisions of the program will be communicated on an as-needed basis to either the workforce as a whole or to the affected specific departments.

The requirement for the biannual completion and/or revision of the anti-fraud program will result in this biannual training schedule to restart every two years.

Continuous Fraud Awareness Training

Quarterly Awareness Training

The company will provide quarterly companywide training that covers various areas as identified below to raise awareness of the definition of fraud, fraud trends, what can occur, what can be done about it, and what the company has done to address these issues of fraud.

- Fraud definition
- Fraud types
- Fraud trends
- Fraud costs
- Industry-specific fraud issues
- Fraud indicators for the company
- Fraud reporting policy
- Suggestions for improvements in control activities

Comments: This training should be designed to be broad in nature to cover overall fraud education, as indicated by the first four bullet points, and then move to industry- and company-specific fraud issues, such as indicated by the last four bullet points.

I emphasize that every training session should include a reminder that the company has established a fraud reporting policy for the benefit of its employees. The full policy does not have to be reviewed in detail to be effective. The purpose of the reminder is to review the purpose of the policy. This simple reminder will serve to keep the policy fresh in the minds of the employees.

Finally, these sessions should include soliciting from the workforce any comments or suggestions they may have for changing or improving the program and the control activities within the program.

Annual Fraud Awareness Training Content Requirements

With quarterly training covering various topics, it would appear that most areas of fraud awareness are covered. However, several specific issues must be addressed at least once each year:

- **Review and reacknowledgment of the fraud policy:** Previously in this book, I told the story of what happens when the fraud policy is signed as acknowledged, then never seen again. It is forgotten. As a result, the fraud policy represents one of the policies that must be reviewed at least once a year. After the review, each employee must be required to acknowledge the policy with an updated signature.
- **Review and reacknowledgment of the fraud reporting policy:** This policy should also be reviewed and reacknowledged on an annual basis. The purpose for this annual requirement is exactly the same as for the fraud policy. The primary reason for this policy is to let the workforce know that the company cares about them and their feelings. Again, there is nothing more detrimental to the mental well-being of an employee than to know or suspect fraud is occurring and to be unable to tell someone.
- **Annual recompletion of the conflict of interest form:** Chapter 6 presented the need for all employees, owners, and governing body members to complete this form annually to guard against any potential conflicts of interest that may arise in considering awarding contracts or even determining the companies that the organization does business with. The new vendor establishment process presented in Chapter 8 also solicits this type of information for the same purpose. This type of information is subject to frequent changes and must be maintained on a current basis to be a valid control activity.

Other Potential Training Topics

Internal Audit Department—Increasing the Perception of Detection

It is understood that not every organization is of the staff size necessary to support a fully functioning internal audit department. Specific issues related to the presence of an internal audit department were presented previously in this book. For purposes of training topics, one issue is re-presented as follows:

- **Communicate the contents of the internal audit work plan, regardless of whether it will all be completed:** Recall that *increasing the perception of detection* is the number one fraud prevention control activity. Even if all of the procedures and audits called for in the internal audit work plan are not performed each year, the perception is that they are being performed. As a result, the perception of detection has increased.

The Visiting Fraud Perpetrator—"It's Just Not Worth It"

As I said previously, management pushed back some when we were required by auditing standards to ask employees about fraud. "Don't give them any ideas," they would say. Now I'm recommending a potential training topic that actually places a convicted fraud perpetrator directly in front of the workforce. "Why is this a good idea?" you ask.

Each year, the Association of Certified Fraud Examiners presents the Global Fraud Conference as its main training opportunity. Thousands of individuals attend the conference each year. Included on the slate of professional presenters are several professional fraudsters, those who have committed and been convicted of the highest profile frauds of recent history. My opinion is that hearing their stories straight from them is one of the most effective deterrents possible. Hearing them tell their stories in their own words and with their own voice inflections and paralinguistics gives you the picture of how they really felt during the perpetration of the fraud. Someone telling another person's story cannot possibly convey those feelings.

In my practice, I am involved in my fraud cases from the investigation to the ultimate conviction by a judge or jury. After 30 years, I have yet to have one of these perpetrators tell me it was worth it. Even the frauds that involved hundreds of millions of dollars don't seem to include perpetrators who ultimately thought it was worth it. The remorse, the guilt, the family members left in their wake, the panic, the sleepless nights—these are the details important to hear.

The situations that leave me shaking my head the most are the small-dollar frauds, the frauds that in no way provide any financial comfort for the perpetrator. These individuals have completely given away everything in a career for pennies. These are the stories that the workforce needs to hear.

• • •

Based on the information included in this chapter, it is apparent that the communication—the company fraud training program element of the anti-fraud program—is one of the most important. A properly designed training program will not result in teaching employees how to do it. Try it. You will see that it raises awareness to a level of prevention and deterrence unachievable in its absence.

12

The Roof

Monitoring and Routine Maintenance

Trust but verify.

—*President Ronald Reagan*

THE FINAL STRUCTURAL ELEMENT of the anti-fraud program is monitoring and routine maintenance. A roof on a home protects the structure from the outside elements. In the same manner, the roof of our anti-fraud program, the monitoring and routine maintenance element, protects the structure through determining its stability (compliance with the program) and identifying areas in need of routine maintenance to keep the structure solid.

Imagine that you have finished building a home, moved in, and enjoyed several years of living in the fruits of your labor. One evening, you're sitting in your living room watching television when you feel a drop of rain on your head. You look up and notice that you can see the sky through numerous holes in the roof. You say to yourself, "How on earth did that happen? I painstakingly built this home from the ground up. I laid the foundation, put in the floor, raised the walls, and weathered it in with the ceiling and the roof. Oh wait, I never had the home inspected and tested for soundness, and I really haven't put any money into routine maintenance." As you sit there getting wetter by the minute, you realize that it may be too late. Now you may have to start over and rebuild, this time the right way.

Such is the case with an anti-fraud program that has no monitoring and routine maintenance element. This element provides the very measure of stability and soundness and the necessary routine maintenance that is critical to the long-term effectiveness of the program.

As part of the nuclear arms treaty negotiations between Ronald Reagan and Mikhail Gorbachev, President Reagan coined the phrase "trust but verify." He knew the importance of trust in a relationship but also understood that a certain amount of verification was needed in order to validate that trust. As I have already stated, I constantly hear statements from victims of fraud such as "but we trusted him." Yes, trust is good; blind trust is not. This element of the anti-fraud program provides the verification needed to validate that trust.

 ## MONITORING AND ROUTINE MAINTENANCE DEFINED

Simply stated, monitoring and routine maintenance is the process of auditing for compliance that results in the ability to determine and implement necessary modifications to the program (routine maintenance) to make it stronger, more efficient, and more effective.

The procedures performed in this element help to answer the questions

- How are things working out?
- Are processes and controls operating as intended?
- Are there processes or activities that we need to refine, add, or delete?

As with any question, we won't know the answer unless we ask. This element requires asking the questions. Unfortunately, I frequently encounter organizations that have beautifully executed the process of anti-fraud program design but ignore or overlook this element. Their anti-fraud program is as beneficial as a house full of holes.

 ## THE MONITORING AND ROUTINE MAINTENANCE STRUCTURE

A sound monitoring structure includes two aspects:

1. Compliance audits
2. Continuous amendments/routine maintenance

Compliance Audits

The Design

As noted throughout the anti-fraud program, certain audits for compliance must be performed on a periodic basis. A compliance audit is not a high-level auditing discipline. In this context, a compliance audit is basically performing certain procedures to determine that the control activity is being done properly.

Recall that our control activities for paper check disbursements require that the authorized check signer review all supporting documentation for a check before signing the check. Once reviewed for agreement of amount and validity of the business purpose, the documentation is to be initialed by the check signer as done and in agreement.

To test compliance with this control activity, the compliance audit procedures may be reflected in these four steps:

1. Obtain a list of disbursements for the recent month.
2. Select 20 disbursements from this list for compliance review.
3. Obtain the supporting documentation (check copy and invoice or other supporting documentation) for each of the 20 disbursements.
4. Determine the following for the 20 disbursements:
   - Check amount agrees with supporting documentation.
   - Documentation supports a valid business purpose.
   - Supporting documentation has been initialed by authorized check signer.

A completed sample compliance audit program for this control activity can be structured as shown in Figure 12.1.

The actual compliance audit working paper can be structured as shown in Figure 12.2.

Once completed, the compliance audit program and the compliance audit working paper should be forwarded to management, per the requirements of the anti-fraud program, for review and determination of whether follow-up actions are necessary. Per this sample working paper, no exceptions were noted. However, for purposes of illustration, assume there were exceptions. Management would then make a determination as to whether follow-up actions are necessary, such as employee discipline or retraining. Documentation of the follow-up actions will be noted on the "management response" section of the compliance audit program as reflected in Figure 12.1.

COMPLIANCE AUDIT PROGRAM Control Activity: Authorized Check Signer Approval				
Item #	Procedure	Perf. By	Date	Comments
1.	Obtain a list of disbursements for the current month.	SD	10/12	See working paper C3
2.	Select 20 disbursements from this list for compliance review.	SD	10/12	
3.	Obtain the supporting documentation for each of the selected disbursements.	SD	10/12	
4.	Determine the following for each of the selected disbursements:			
	a) Check amount agrees to supporting documentation	SD	10/12	No exceptions
	b) Documentation supports a valid business purpose	SD	10/12	No exceptions
	c) Supporting documentation has been initialed by authorized check signer	SD	10/12	No exceptions

Management Response:

Were exceptions noted?   <u>No</u>

If yes, document the response to these exceptions below:

<u>Example:</u>

<u>Jeff, the authorized check signer, did not initial as approved for 11 of the 20</u>
<u>disbursements tested. This compliance audit will be reviewed with Jeff as a</u>
<u>matter of retraining. Jeff will receive a formal reprimand related to lack of compliance</u>
<u>with the control activities as noted in the Company Anti-Fraud Program.</u>

Management Signature: _____

Date: _____

Management's Title: _____

FIGURE 12.1 Compliance Audit Program

MED ENTERPRISES, INC.								C3

MED ENTERPRISES, INC.
Compliance Testing Performed by: SD
Control Activity: Authorized Check Signer Approval

Month Tested: September

Disb #	Date	Amount	Payee	Support Doc.	1	2	3	Exceptions
1	9/4/20xx	432.96	BethAnn's Bakery	Yes	✓	✓	✓	None
2	9/6/20xx	1,843.00	Bob's Tires	Yes	✓	✓	✓	None
3	9/8/20xx	1,619.04	Walmart	Yes	✓	✓	✓	None
4	9/14/20xx	660.00	Larry's Copiers	Yes	✓	✓	✓	None
5	9/14/20xx	2,814.00	First Bank	Yes	✓	✓	✓	None
6	9/16/20xx	911.14	Office Supply Barn	Yes	✓	✓	✓	None
7	9/19/20xx	1,212.93	Walmart	Yes	✓	✓	✓	None
8	9/19/20xx	920.62	Jeff's Interiors	Yes	✓	✓	✓	None
9	9/20/20xx	322.64	Cell Phones R Us	Yes	✓	✓	✓	None
10	9/21/20xx	617.87	Electric Co.	Yes	✓	✓	✓	None
11	9/21/20xx	78.89	Kinko's Copies	Yes	✓	✓	✓	None
12	9/23/20xx	916.91	Harold's Foods	Yes	✓	✓	✓	None
13	9/23/20xx	95.05	Federal Express	Yes	✓	✓	✓	None
14	9/25/20xx	1,412.14	First Bank	Yes	✓	✓	✓	None
15	9/26/20xx	836.99	Walmart	Yes	✓	✓	✓	None
16	9/26/20xx	43.01	Bill's Bills	Yes	✓	✓	✓	None
17	9/26/20xx	6.18	Hallmark	Yes	✓	✓	✓	None
18	9/28/20xx	7,443.88	Rick's Plumbing	Yes	✓	✓	✓	None
19	9/29/20xx	18.00	Rona's Flowers	Yes	✓	✓	✓	None
20	9/30/20xx	139.34	CableCom	Yes	✓	✓	✓	None

Attributes Tested:
1   Check amount agrees to supporting documentation
2   Documentation supports a valid business purpose
3   Supporting documentation has been initialed by authorized check signer

FIGURE 12.2 Compliance Audit Working Paper

So with this example, we have asked and answered the three questions as follows:

Q: *"How are things working out?"*

A: Good.

Q: *"Are processes and controls operating as intended?"*

A: Yes.

Q: *"Are there processes or activities that we need to refine, add, or delete?"*

A: No.

A: Or, in the case of the audit that noted certain exceptions, the answer would obviously be yes.

Once all compliance audits have been completed, management should report monthly to the governing body or owner regarding the results. It is absolutely mandatory that these responsible parties stay informed regarding the effectiveness of the anti-fraud program.

Who Should Perform the Compliance Audits?

A question asked quite often is "Who should perform these compliance audits?" This is an extremely important question, the answers to which can be quite diverse. If the organization is large enough to employ its own internal audit department, the task should be assigned here. For those without an internal audit department, an employee confident in performing these specific reviews may be given the responsibility. In no circumstance, however, should that employee ever be put in the position of auditing his or her own area or work. Therefore, in most cases, more than one employee will be performing the compliance audits. Ideally, compliance audits will be performed by employees of the organization; this, of course, is less expensive. However, in some circumstances, the volume of compliance auditing required on a monthly basis dictates hiring someone from outside the organization. If contracting your compliance auditing outside your business becomes too expensive, you are probably ready to establish your own in-house internal audit department.

The Schedule

As noted in the design of the specific control activities, certain control activities must be audited periodically. This list is certainly not all-inclusive. The list provides an example of those control activities that I believe should be subjected to compliance auditing. This list will obviously be different for each specific organization, based on their size, structure, and level of complexity of operations.

It is important to establish the schedule of compliance auditing in the anti-fraud program. As such, the following represents an example schedule that accomplishes this objective:

Monthly Audits
1. Authorized check signer approval.
2. **Approved accounts receivable charge-offs:** As outlined in this control activity area, the comparison of amounts charged off from accounts receivable accounts should be validated against an approved charge-off report provided by the governing body or owner of the organization.
3. **Approved inventory write-offs and adjustments:** The purposes and reasons for this type of compliance audit mirror those of the accounts receivable charge-off scenario. The ability to conceal fraud in these areas is substantial.
4. **Journal entry supporting documentation and approval requirements:** As presented in Chapter 8, the ability to post a journal entry to the accounting records with no related controls provides the perpetrator of fraud an unlimited ability to conceal fraud. Therefore, adherence to these specific control activities is crucial to having an effective anti-fraud program.

Semiannual Audits
5. **Investment audit:** On a semiannual basis, the investment purchase confirmations shall be reviewed for outstanding investments, and safekeeping receipts shall be reviewed for determination that the investment is in the name of the company.

Annual Audits
6. **Master vendor file audit:** As presented in Chapter 8, the need for the new vendor establishment control activities is critical to preventing shell company types of frauds. The control activities for this control process are specific and were developed to reduce the ability to commit this normally high-dollar type of fraud. Accordingly, compliance auditing directed at adherence to these control activities is mandatory.
7. **Contract procurement audit:** On an annual basis, all known contracts executed within the current year shall be audited for compliance with the competitive bid requirements outlined in the Control Activities for this control area.

8. **Large disbursements audit:** A list of disbursements that exceed $25,000 shall be produced and reviewed for evidence that dual signatures were included on the checks and competitive bids were obtained for items for which competitive bids should have been obtained.

These specific compliance audit requirements represent those areas that should always be included as part of the monitoring and routine maintenance element of an effective anti-fraud program. Additional specific compliance audits may be performed at the discretion of management as determined necessary.

Continuous Amendments/Routine Maintenance

A process that identifies areas that are in need of improvement or amendment is absolutely necessary. This element establishes that process. The compliance auditing function identifies areas where there may be problems with the control activities. In analyzing these problems, the cause of these exceptions or instances of noncompliance must be determined as follows:

- Cause: Human error or noncompliance
- Cause: Design error in the control activity

The consequences of human error or noncompliance have previously been addressed. For those issues of noncompliance that are caused by a flaw in the design of the control activity, we know we have redesign issues (routine maintenance) to consider.

Additionally, it should be recognized that the employees responsible for carrying out specific control activities are sometimes in the best position to offer suggestions for improvements to control activities. As such, employees should be part of a process that encourages submission of any suggestions for improvement.

To accomplish the objective of routine maintenance, the following requirements should be included in the anti-fraud program:

- On an annual basis, the control activities development team shall review the results of all specific compliance audits to determine what amendments, additions, and/or deletions shall be implemented, if any.
- On an annual basis, the control activities development team shall interview each employee regarding their specific areas of responsibility to solicit their input into how well the control activities are operating and any comments or suggestions they may have for improvement.

Based on the conclusions reached about these control activities reviews, the control activities development team shall revise or add new control activities forms as amendments to this anti-fraud program.

• • •

In summary, it is evident that the structure needs a roof, and the roof should be maintained. The monitoring and routine maintenance element of the anti-fraud program should therefore be designed to test the stability of the structure, and the results can then be used to determine where to direct the routine maintenance.

CHAPTER THIRTEEN

The Sample Anti-Fraud Program

S IMPLE PRACTICALITY IS the goal we set out to accomplish. The design of an effective and efficient anti-fraud program doesn't have to be difficult. It should be simple and practical. I believe we have accomplished that objective.

We laid a solid foundation (environment), installed the floor (risk assessment), raised the walls (control activities), put in the ceiling (information and communication), and topped it off with the roof (monitoring).

You've worked hard. Enjoy living in the fruits of your labor!

MED ENTERPRISES, INC. COMPANY ANTI-FRAUD PROGRAM

Introduction

T he board of directors of MED Enterprises, Inc. (the "Company") has established this program to address the risk associated with internal fraud. Internal fraud is defined as fraud perpetrated against the Company by our own employees. The purpose also includes the establishment of an environment that promotes and recognizes honesty and integrity in the workforce and a safe and pleasant working atmosphere.

(continued)

Internal fraud includes three types of fraud: misappropriation, corruption, and financial statement fraud, illustrated as follows:

1. **Misappropriation:** This is defined as the taking of company assets whether cash, inventory, or other fixed assets. This is the most common type of fraud.

2. **Corruption:** This type of fraud is represented by collusion between at least two individuals (one employee and a nonemployee or two employees), including conflicts of interest in purchasing and sales schemes, bribery in kickbacks and bid-rigging schemes, illegal gratuities, and economic extortion.

3. **Financial statement fraud:** This fraud includes the intentional misrepresentation of the financial position or results of operations of the Company.

POLICIES OF PROTECTION

Certain policies have been established that provide protection for not only the Company but for each employee as well. On the date of employment, each employee will receive an employee manual that includes the complete text of policies established by the board of directors. As relates to fraud, the following three policies have been adopted:

Fraud Policy

We want you to know that we take the issue of internal fraud seriously. We have adopted a no tolerance position regarding fraud occurrences and desire that the workforce joins us in this level of dedication to fraud prevention and detection. This policy was adopted to provide information about fraud, what to do if you suspect fraud, and our obligations to investigate suspicions of fraud. The policy also outlines the administrative actions that will be applied if you are suspected of the perpetration of internal fraud.

Fraud Reporting Policy

This policy was adopted to provide you with the opportunity to anonymously report suspicions of fraud. A healthy workforce is the result of your feeling as if you have someone to turn to in reporting suspicions. The policy outlines the process to follow in reporting any suspicions and our responsibilities to investigate these issues.

Expense Reimbursement Policy

The protection of and accountability for Company funds is of prime importance to us. We recognize that needs often arise for the use of Company funds for various purposes, such as travel and other purchasing needs. This policy was established to provide a sound accountability framework that ensures proper reporting, as well as protection for you, the employee.

FRAUD AWARENESS TRAINING

As a governing body or owners, we commit to you that continuous fraud awareness training covering the topics addressed in this anti-fraud program will be conducted. Additionally, we will ensure that continuous fraud awareness training is conducted that covers current fraud trends and the importance of fraud prevention and detection. The intent of the training is to partner with you in all aspects of fraud prevention, resulting in a safe and sound working environment. Specifics of the fraud awareness training aspect of the anti-fraud program will be addressed in detail later in this program.

FRAUD RISK ASSESSMENT

Introduction

A formal fraud risk assessment process is required by this anti-fraud program. The fraud risk assessment is to be performed biannually by the fraud risk assessment team as identified here.

The purpose of the fraud risk assessment process is to identify those areas of transaction performance and recording that are most vulnerable to fraud. Control activities to address these identified areas are developed by the control activities development team as identified in the control activities section of this program.

Fraud Risk Assessment Team

The fraud risk assessment team shall include the following staff positions:

Management (executive and middle)

Accounting supervisor

(continued)

Sales manager

Human resources manager

Billing supervisor

Customer service manager

In-house legal counsel

The risk assessment team shall conduct the biannual risk assessment meetings over a three-week time period in April of the applicable year. The team shall appoint a facilitator from among the team members for the purpose of scheduling and organizing the content of the meetings.

The fraud risk assessment shall be documented, utilizing the fraud risk assessment framework included as Appendix A to this program.

Once completed, the fraud risk assessment framework shall be provided to the control activities development team to serve as a guide for the performance of their responsibilities as defined.

Though the risk assessment team is only required to perform the assessment on a biannual basis, team members should be aware of operational changes that could result in additional vulnerabilities to fraud.

The facilitator of the risk assessment team shall inform executive management of any new vulnerabilities that may be identified in between fraud risk assessments. Executive management has the responsibility to present these new vulnerabilities to the control activities development team for inclusion in the anti-fraud program if determined necessary.

CONTROL ACTIVITIES

Introduction

Control activities are defined as those activities, controls, checks and balances, and processes that have been implemented to address the risks of internal fraud in our Company.

A control activity can be as simple as the requirement for two authorized signatures on checks over a certain dollar amount and as complex as a complete policy, such as the expense reimbursement policy.

Control Activities Development Team

The control activities development team shall include the following staff positions:

Executive management

Accounting supervisor

In-house legal counsel

Upon receipt of the fraud risk assessment framework, the team shall develop certain and specific control activities that address the identified fraud risks. Control activities shall be documented using the control activities form included as Appendix B to this program.

Communication of Control Activities

The complete anti-fraud program, including specific control activities, will be issued in its entirety at the biannual deadline of June 1, utilizing the following means of communication:

Electronic distribution: Company intranet, e-mail

Print distribution: As part of this anti-fraud program

Continuous training: As directed by this program

The level of communication and training related to control activities will be conducted to ensure a thorough understanding of the requirements imposed upon all staff positions.

Compliance with Control Activities

Control activities have been developed over time with an extensive amount of effort. It is required that control activities as apply to your specific position will be followed. We encourage staff to ask questions if there is a lack of understanding of any control activity. Failure to adhere to the various control activities will result in the following:

First violation: Formal reprimand and retraining if necessary

Second violation: Termination

As part of the ongoing monitoring aspect of this program, we encourage you to submit to executive management any suggestions you may have for improving specific control activities.

Specific Control Activities

Specific control activities that have been placed into operation are included as Appendix C to this program.

COMMUNICATION: THE COMPANY TRAINING PROGRAM

Because of the importance we place on this anti-fraud program and overall fraud awareness, the following program distribution and training schedule will apply:

Anti-Fraud Program Training

June 1 (biannually): Distribution of the Anti-Fraud Program to the Workforce

The anti-fraud program will be made available on the Company intranet and will be provided electronically to your e-mail inbox. Additionally, a printed copy of the program will be provided for each employee.

By June 15 (biannually): Companywide Training on the Anti-Fraud Program

Within the two-week time period after the distribution of the anti-fraud program, the Company will conduct specific training on all aspects of the program to all employees.

By July 15 (biannually): Departmental Related Specific Control Activities Training

During the four-week time period following the presentation of the new anti-fraud program, the Company will conduct training regarding specific control activities related to the respective departments.

All companywide and departmental specific anti-fraud program training will be completed by July 15 on a biannual basis, at which time the anti-fraud program will be considered operating in full effect.

Continuous Fraud Awareness Training

The Company will provide quarterly training that covers various areas, as identified here, to raise awareness of fraud and fraud-related issues.

General Fraud Training

Fraud definition

Fraud types

Fraud trends

Fraud costs

Company-Specific Fraud Training

Industry-specific fraud issues

Fraud indicators for the Company

Fraud reporting policy

Suggestions for improvements in control activities

During the interim year between fraud risk assessments, company-wide training will be conducted that includes information considered to be new or updated. Additionally, the annual training will include a review of the fraud policy, the fraud reporting policy, and the conflict of interest form. At the conclusion of this review, all employees will be required to sign the acknowledgment of understanding for these two policies and complete an updated conflict of interest form.

MONITORING

Compliance Auditing and Routine Maintenance

The governing body or owner is committed to providing the most effective and efficient anti-fraud program possible. This can result only from periodic auditing for compliance with the various control activities provisions and a system of process review.

It is understood that the design of specific control activities may need to be revised, based on issues that employees encounter while performing the activity. This process can result in revisions, additions to, or deletions of certain control activities. This process of revision thus represents a maintenance process for the control activities that are a part of the overall anti-fraud program.

The employees responsible for carrying out specific control activities are sometimes in the best position to offer suggestions for improvements to control activities. As such, employees are encouraged to submit any suggestions, in writing, to the executive management of the company.

Compliance Audits

As noted throughout the anti-fraud program, certain audits for compliance must be performed on a periodic basis. Compliance audit programs and audit working papers (included as Appendix D) shall be submitted to management for possible follow-up activities. The results of the various compliance audits shall be submitted to the governing body or owner for review.

(continued)

The schedule of mandated compliance audits is as follows:

Monthly Audits

Authorized check signer approval

Approved accounts receivable charge-offs

Approved inventory write-offs and adjustments

Journal entry supporting documentation and approval requirements

Semiannual Audit

Investment audit

Annual Audits

Master vendor file audit

Contract procurement audit

Large disbursements audit

Additional specific compliance audits may be performed at the discretion of management as determined necessary.

Continuous Amendments—Routine Maintenance

To accomplish the objective of routine maintenance, the following processes will be conducted:

On an annual basis, the control activities development team shall review the results of all specific compliance audits to determine what amendments, additions, and/or deletions shall be implemented, if any.

On an annual basis, the control activities development team shall interview each employee regarding their specific areas of responsibility to solicit their input into how well the control activities are operating and any comments or suggestions they may have for improvement.

Based on the conclusions reached about these control activities reviews, the control activities development team shall revise or add new control activities forms as amendments to this anti-fraud program.

APPENDIX 13A: FRAUD RISK ASSESSMENT FRAMEWORK FORM

Identified Fraud Risks and Schemes	Likelihood	Financial Significance	Risk No. Ref.

FIGURE 13A.1 Fraud Risk Assessment Framework Form (Blank)

APPENDIX 13B: CONTROL ACTIVITIES FORM

Company Name:
Anti-Fraud Program
Documentation of Control Activities
Dated:

Control Activity	Control Activities																
1																	
2																	
3																	
4																	
5																	
6																	
7																	
8																	
9																	
10																	
11																	
12																	
13																	
14																	
15																	

FIGURE 13B.1 Control Activities Form (Blank)

APPENDIX 13C: DOCUMENTATION OF CONTROL ACTIVITIES

MED ENTERPRISES, INC.
Anti-Fraud Program
Documentation of Control Activities
Dated: September 16, 20xx

Control Activities

Accounts Receivable Daily Work

1	The cashier completes the "daily cash receipts" sheet and prepares the deposit slip.
2	The completed cash sheet is then forwarded to accounts receivable clerk 1, who posts the payments to the individual customer accounts.
3	Accounts receivable clerk 1 then runs a "daily batch summary" on accounts receivable postings.
4	The bank bag with money and the completed deposit slip will be forwarded by the cashier to accounts receivable clerk 2.
5	Accounts receivable clerk 2 takes the deposit to the bank and obtains the validated deposit slip.
6	Upon return, accounts receivable clerk 2 forwards the validated deposit slip to accounts receivable clerk 1, who compares and agrees the validated deposit slip to the total of the "daily batch summary" of accounts receivable postings and initials as in agreement.
7	Accounts receivable clerk 1 then files the "daily cash sheet," the "daily batch summary," and the "validated deposit slip" together in the daily work file.

FIGURE 13C.1   Accounts Receivable Daily Work

MED ENTERPRISES, INC.
Anti-Fraud Program
Documentation of Control Activities
Dated: September 16, 20xx

Control Activities
Reasonable Method for the Determination of the Adequacy of the Allowance for Uncollectible Accounts
1 The calculation of the desired balance in the Allowance for Uncollectible Accounts will be performed at the end of each month by the accounting supervisor prior to preparation of the month-end closing journal entries.
2 The journal entry to adjust the allowance account will be prepared and submitted for approval by management. Note: This journal entry is subject to the provisions of the controls surrounding all journal entries.
3 Once approved, the journal entry will be posted by accounting clerk 1.

FIGURE 13C.2   Reasonable Method for the Determination of the Adequacy of the Allowance for Uncollectible Accounts

MED ENTERPRISES, INC.
Anti-Fraud Program
Documentation of Control Activities
Dated: September 16, 20xx

Control Activities

Required Approval for Charge-Offs

1	Board of directors approval is required for any and all charge-offs.
2	Prior to the monthly board meetings, management will meet with the collections department to discuss the status of delinquent accounts and determine which accounts should be submitted for charge-off approval.
3	The collections department will prepare a written charge-off report complete with account number, name, and account balance for submission to the board for approval.
4	After discussion in the board of directors meeting, approval will be given for the charge-off accounts.
5	Management will forward the Approved Charge-Off Report to the accounting department for preparation and posting of the charge off journal entry.
6	Prior to the subsequent month's board of directors meeting, management will review this charge-off report to the general ledger activity where the charge-offs were recorded and initial as in agreement.
7	Any differences or deviations from the previously agreed-upon amounts or accounts to what is recorded will be immediately investigated and resolved.

FIGURE 13C.3 Required Approval for Charge-Offs

MED ENTERPRISES, INC.
Anti-Fraud Program
Documentation of Control Activities
Dated: September 16, 20xx

	Control Activities
Investments	
1	Investments are to be purchased in the name of the company only.
2	Investment sales and purchases will occur only on approval of the investment committee.
3	CUSIP confirmation slips for purchases and sales will be retained by the accounting department.
4	The accounting supervisor will prepare a month-end investment report and submit to management and/or the board of directors for monthly review.
5	As part of the formal monitoring program, to verify compliance with control activities, a review of the listed investments against the safekeeping information and CUSIP confirmation information will be performed semi-annually by the responsible party.

FIGURE 13C.4 Investments

MED ENTERPRISES, INC.
Anti-Fraud Program
Documentation of Control Activities
Dated: September 16, 20xx

	Control Activities
	Warehouse Inventory and Periodic Inventory Counts
1	Access to the inventory locations will be locked after hours and under the control of the custodian of the warehouse.
2	Access to the inventory locations will be approved by the warehouseman during business hours.
3	Inventory will be issued from the warehouse only upon presentation of a properly completed and authorized Inventory Issue Request form.
4	Inventory returns require an Inventory Return slip, which provides the item number, condition, and original issue value.
5	At the end of each quarter, the accounting department will produce a perpetual inventory report count sheet, which provides the item number and quantity on hand that exists in the accounting records.
6	Accounting clerk 2 and the senior warehouseman will take the perpetual inventory count sheet to perform a physical count of the inventory on hand, noting the actual count of items on hand next to the perpetual record number of items on hand.
7	Accounting clerk 2 and the warehouseman will both initial the count as complete.
8	Accounting clerk 2 will then forward the count sheet to accounting clerk 1, who will input the physical count numbers into the perpetual inventory count system in order to produce an Inventory Variance Report.
9	For those items with significant variances, accounting clerk 2 and the senior warehouseman will perform a recount; explanations will have to be provided for any inventory differences.
10	Once the counts are double-verified, accounting clerk 1 will run the final inventory variance report and prepare the necessary adjusting journal entry to record the inventory difference (overage or shortage).
11	The system will automatically update the perpetual inventory system with the new final counts and values.

FIGURE 13C.5   Warehouse Inventory and Periodic Inventory Counts

MED ENTERPRISES, INC.
Anti-Fraud Program
Documentation of Control Activities
Dated: September 16, 20xx

	Control Activities
	Physical Controls over Warehouse Inventory and Capitalized Equipment
1	Access to the inventory locations will be locked after hours and under the control of the custodian of the warehouse.
2	Access to the inventory locations will be approved by the warehouseman during business hours.
3	The personal use of company fixed assets and inventory will be determined by management on a case-by-case basis.
4	The proper Request for Personal Use form will be completed by the requesting employee and submitted to management.
5	Management will either approve or deny the request based on various factors such as level of planned personal use, length of time needed for personal use, and upcoming planned business use of the asset.
6	If approved, the asset will be checked out with a completed "check out slip" prepared by the warehouseman and will be inspected by the warehouseman upon return to the warehouse.
7	A "return slip" will be prepared by the warehouseman and signed by the employee returning the equipment.
8	The "return slip" will be forwarded to management while a copy of the return slip will be placed in the employee's personnel file.

FIGURE 13C.6 Physical Controls over Warehouse Inventory and Capitalized Equipment

MED ENTERPRISES, INC.
Anti-Fraud Program
Documentation of Control Activities
Dated: September 16, 20xx

	Control Activities
	Approval for Inventory Write-Offs
1	The determination of inventory obsolescence shall be performed on a quarterly basis.
2	The warehouseman and accounting clerk 1 should review inventory on hand for those items that are old, damaged, or otherwise not acceptable for sale or use.
3	Accounting clerk 1 shall prepare an inventory obsolescence report that provides the item number, description, and number of items that are considered obsolete.
4	The warehouseman and accounting clerk 1 should both initial this report as complete and forward it to accounting clerk 2.
5	Accounting clerk 2 will perform the cost times quantity extension calculations that will then be placed on the Inventory Write-off Valuation Report.
6	The Inventory Write-off Valuation Report should then be submitted to the board of directors for approval.
7	The approved Inventory Write-off Valuation Report should then be forwarded to the accounting department for preparation and posting of the write-off journal entry.

FIGURE 13C.7 Approval for Inventory Write-Offs

MED ENTERPRISES, INC.
Anti-Fraud Program
Documentation of Control Activities
Dated: September 16, 20xx

Control Activities

Payroll Processing

1	A criminal background check and reference checking will be part of the hiring process.

2	A personnel file will be maintained for each employee, which may include:
	    Background checks
	    Resume
	    Authorization for salary or rate of pay
	        Reference checks
	        Identifying information (copies of driver's license and Social Security card)

3	Information regarding name, address, Social Security number, and authorized rate of pay will be entered into the payroll processing system by accounting clerk 1.
4	Addresses, Social Security numbers, and driver's license numbers will be cross-referenced with existing employees for purposes of identifying potential ghost employees.
5	Hourly employees will be required to prepare regular time sheets to be submitted to their supervisor for review and approval.
6	Once approved, time sheets will be forwarded to accounting clerk 2 for entry of hours worked into the payroll processing system.
7	Accounting clerk 2 will also review commission calculation forms for accuracy.
8	Once the hours and commissions payable are entered into the payroll processing system, an initial payroll register for the period will be produced and forwarded to accounting clerk 1.
9	Accounting clerk 1 will review the list of employees paid against a list of company employees and initial as in agreement.

10	Accounting clerk 1 will review the initial payroll register for reasonableness of the pay amounts, looking for input errors that may have occurred.
11	Accounting clerk 1 will initial the register and return to accounting clerk 2.
12	Accounting clerk 2, only on presentation of an approved payroll register from accounting clerk 1, will finalize the payroll register, which results in the preparation of the paychecks or direct deposit file.
13	For paper checks, the control activities surrounding the paper check disbursement process will apply.
14	For direct deposit, the direct deposit file will be forwarded to the authorized check signer, and the control activities surrounding the electronic disbursement process will apply.
15	For paper checks, the paychecks will be distributed to the employees by the accounting supervisor, who has no part in the process of the production of paychecks.
16	If not directly interfaced, accounting clerk 2 will post the payroll register information to the general ledger.
17	The accounting supervisor will review the posting of the payroll against the payroll register information and initial as in agreement.

FIGURE 13C.8 Payroll Processing

MED ENTERPRISES, INC.
Anti-Fraud Program
Documentation of Control Activities
Dated: September 16, 20xx

	Control Activities
	Competitive Bid Process for Contract Procurement
1	On an annual basis, all employees will complete the Conflicts of Interest Form, detailing the nature of any business relationships or conflicts, familial or ownership or both, they could potentially have with suppliers and service providers.
2	Disbursements that are anticipated to exceed $25,000 must be approved by the board of directors.
3	Contracts or disbursements anticipated to exceed $30,000 are subject to the competitive bidding process as outlined below.

4	Competitive bidding requirements for contracts or disbursements anticipated to exceed $30,000 include the following:
	  Bidding requirements will be determined by the applicable department head
	  The bid requirements will be advertised upon approval of management
	  A minimum of three sealed bids will be required
	  Sealed bids will be opened after the deadline and evaluated for various criteria, such as cost, compliance with bid requirements, and bondability.
	  The accepted bid contract or invoice will be signed by management after ratification by the board of directors.

5	As part of the formal monitoring program, for compliance with these control activities, a review of the contracts awarded or disbursements made in excess of $25,000 will be audited annually by the responsible party.

FIGURE 13C.9 Competitive Bid Process for Contract Procurement

MED ENTERPRISES, INC.
Anti-Fraud Program
Documentation of Control Activities
Dated: September 16, 20xx

	Control Activities
Journal Entries	
1	Every nonstandard journal entry requires the completion of a Journal Entry Voucher.
2	Documentation that supports the nature, reason, and amount of the journal entry should be attached to the Journal Entry Voucher.
3	Journal Entry Vouchers shall be forwarded to the accounting supervisor for review and approval by initialing.
4	Journal Entry Vouchers initialed by the accounting supervisor shall be forwarded to and approved by management.
5	Once approved, the Journal Entry Vouchers shall be forwarded to accounting clerk 1 or accounting clerk 2 for posting to the general ledger.
6	Journal entries will not be posted to the general ledger without the approved documentation attached to the approved Journal Entry Voucher.
7	The accounting clerk who posted the journal entry to the general ledger shall initial the approved Journal Entry Voucher.
8	Journal Entry Vouchers and the supporting documentation will be filed numerically in the accounting department files.
9	As part of the formal monitoring program, compliance with the review of the supporting documentation set for the journal entries will be audited monthly to determine the level of adherence to that control activity.

FIGURE 13C.10 Journal Entries

149

MED ENTERPRISES, INC.
Anti-Fraud Program
Documentation of Control Activities
Dated: September 16, 20xx

Control Activities

New Vendor Establishment Procedures

1	A Master Vendor File will be maintained and updated on a regular basis.
2	A New Vendor Establishment Form will be initiated within the accounts payable department for all new vendors.
3	Information to be obtained for the form will be requested from the new vendor and completed by accounts payable clerk 1.
4	Accounts payable clerk 1 will forward the information completed portion of the New Vendor Establishment form to accounts payable clerk 2.
5	Accounts payable clerk 2 will then validate the information on the form. Validation and verification will include: Phone calls to numbers provided Test e-mail message to the e-mail provided Web-based search engine inquiries State tax base searches Online mapping or Google Earth searches of address provided
6	Accounts payable clerk 2 will forward the completed New Vendor Establishment Form to management for approval.
7	The approved New Vendor Establishment form, along with any other documentation from the vendor, will be added to the Master Vendor File.
8	As part of the formal monitoring program, compliance with the review of the supporting documentation and form completion for the Master Vendor File will be audited annually to determine the level of adherence to that control activity.

FIGURE 13C.11 New Vendor Establishment Procedures

150

MED ENTERPRISES, INC.
Anti-Fraud Program
Documentation of Control Activities
Dated: September 16, 20xx

	Control Activities
Disbursements with Paper Checks	
1	The authorized check signers are as follows: Jeff Chapman, Stephan Smith (both signatures required for any disbursement exceeding $25,000)
2	Checks of less than $5,000 only require one signature.
3	Checks equal to or exceeding $5,000 must have the signatures of both of the authorized check signers.
4	Invoices, statements, and/or payment requests are distributed from the incoming mail to the appropriate responsible department head (responsible party).
5	The responsible party compares the invoice to the purchase order and receiving slip to determine agreement.
6	The responsible party then approves the invoice for payment by initialing the invoice as approved.
7	Approved invoices are forwarded to the accounts payable department for general ledger account coding and preparation of the check.
8	The check can only be prepared if there is an approved set of supporting documentation (invoice, monthly statement, payment requests, Expense Report Form, Supplemental Business Meal and Entertainment Charges Documentation Form).
9	The checks, with the supporting documentation attached, are forwarded to the authorized check signer for signature.
10	The authorized check signer must review the check and supporting documentation for each of the following: Check amount agrees to the supporting documentation Supporting documentation reflects that the disbursement is for a valid business purpose
11	Once satisfied, the authorized check signer initials the documentation and signs the check.
12	The authorized check signer forwards the documentation to the accounting department.
13	The accounting department makes a copy of the check and then places the check in an envelope and into the outgoing mail basket.
14	The accounting department files the check copy and the supporting documentation together in the alphabetical invoice filing system.
15	As part of the formal monitoring program, compliance with the review of the supporting documentation set before checks are signed will be audited periodically to determine the level of adherence to that control activity.

FIGURE 13C.12 Disbursements with Paper Checks

MED ENTERPRISES, INC.
Anti-Fraud Program
Documentation of Control Activities
Dated: September 16, 20xx

Control Activities
Bank Reconciliations
1 The senior accountant is responsible for performing the bank reconciliations on a monthly basis.
2 The senior accountant is not to have signature authority on the bank accounts.
3 The bank reconciliations must be completed by the third day of the month and submitted to the accounting supervisor upon completion.
4 The accounting supervisor shall review the bank reconciliations for accuracy and for follow-up issues for uncleared deposits in transit and outstanding checks as necessary.
5 Once satisfied, the accounting supervisor will initial the reconciliation as approved and file in the related company file.

FIGURE 13C.13 Bank Reconciliations

MED ENTERPRISES, INC.
Anti-Fraud Program
Documentation of Control Activities
Dated: September 16, 20xx

	Control Activities
Receipts Process	
1	Incoming mail will be opened by one individual. The individual responsible for opening the mail will rotate weekly and includes the following positions: receptionist, accounting clerk 1, accounting clerk 2.
2	An "incoming mail receipts log" that provides the total of customer payments will be prepared by the individual opening the mail and then forwarded to the cashier, along with the daily collections.
3	The cashier will complete the "daily cash sheet" noting customer name, account number, and amount paid.
4	The cashier will compare the total of the "incoming mail receipts log" to the total per the daily cash sheet and initial as in agreement.
5	The cashier will then prepare the deposit slip from the information noted on the daily cash sheet.
6	The daily cash sheet will be forwarded to accounting clerk 2.
7	The bank bag with the checks and deposit slip will be forwarded to accounting clerk 1, who will take the deposit to the bank and obtain the validated deposit slip.
8	Accounting clerk 2 will post the payments to the individual customer accounts receivable accounts and run a "daily batch summary" of accounts receivable postings.
9	Accounting clerk 1 will bring the validated deposit slip from the bank and forward it to accounting clerk 2.
10	Accounting clerk 2 will compare the daily batch summary of accounts receivable postings to the amount per the validated deposit slip and initial as in agreement.
11	Accounting clerk 2 will file the incoming mail log, the daily cash sheet, the daily batch summary of accounts receivable postings, and the deposit slip in the daily work file for that day.

FIGURE 13C.14 Receipts Process

APPENDIX 13D: COMPLIANCE AUDIT PROGRAMS AND RELATED COMPLIANCE AUDIT WORKING PAPERS

COMPLIANCE AUDIT PROGRAM **Control Activity: Required Approval for Charge-Offs**				
Item # Procedure	Perf. by	Date	Comments	
1. Obtain the general ledger history printout for the charge-off account				
2. Obtain the approved charge-off report from management				
3. Trail amounts posted to the general ledger to the approved charge-off list				
4. Determine the following for each of the charge-offs: a) Evidence that the charge-off report has been initialed by the board of directors b) Name, account number, and amount agrees to supporting documentation c) Name, account number, and amount are on approved charge-off report				

Management Response:

   Were exceptions noted?   _____

   If yes, document the response to these exceptions below:

   Example: _____

_____

_____

_____

_____

_____

Management Signature: _____

Date: _____

Management's Title: _____

FIGURE 13D.1   Approved Charge-Offs Compliance Form

Company Name: _____   Performed by:_____
Compliance Testing
Control Activity: Approval for Charge-Offs

Month Tested: _____

Item	Account Number	Amount	Name	Support Doc.	1	2	3	4	Exceptions

Attributes Tested:
1. Charge-off amount trailed to the appropriate general ledger account
2. Charge-off amount is listed on the "initialed as approved" Charge-Off Report
3. Supporting documentation lists the same account number, name, and amount
4. Charge-Off Report initialed as approved by the board of directors

FIGURE 13D.2   Approved Charge-Offs Compliance Testing

COMPLIANCE AUDIT PROGRAM Control Activity: Investment Audit			
Item # Procedure	Perf. by	Date	Comments
1. Obtain the report of current investments with type, account balance, purchase date, maturity date, and interest rate included			
2. Obtain all supporting documentation regarding purchases and sales of investments for the last six months			
3. Trail all current investments and sales of investments to the month-end investment reports submitted to management			
4. Determine the following for each investment: a) Evidence that all investments are in the name of the company b) Trail approval of purchases and sales to the investment committee minutes obtained as supporting documentation c) Confirm that all investments and sales were presented in the proper month-end investment report to management d) Confirm that all CUSIP slips are filed in the accounting department			

Management Response:

Were exceptions noted? _____

If yes, document the response to these exceptions below:

Example: _____

_____

_____

_____

_____

Management Signature: _____

Date: _____

Management's Title: _____

FIGURE 13D.3 Investments Compliance Form

Company Name:_____

Compliance Testing

Control Activity: Investment Audit

Performed by:_____

Six Months Tested: _____

Item	Investment Type	Name	Account Balance	Maturity Date	1	2	3	4	Exceptions

Attributes Tested:
1. Investment is in the name of the company
2. Purchases and sales trailed to investment committee minutes
3. Purchases and sales trailed to proper month-end investment reports for management
4. CUSIP slip is filed with the accounting department

FIGURE 13D.4 Investments Compliance Testing

COMPLIANCE AUDIT PROGRAM Control Activity: Required Approval for Inventory Write-Offs				
Item #	Procedure	Perf. by	Date	Comments
1.	Obtain the general ledger history printout for the inventory write-off account			
2.	Obtain the Inventory Write-Off Inventory Valuation Report from management			
3.	Trail amounts posted to the general ledger to the approved write-off list			
4.	Determine the following for each of the write-offs: a) Evidence that the write-off report has been initialed by the board of directors b) Item number, description, and number of items agree to general ledger account c) Item number, description, and number of items are on approved write-off report d) Item number, description, and number of items agrees to supporting documentation			

Management Response:

    Were exceptions noted?   _____

    If yes, document the response to these exceptions below:

    Example: _____

    _____

    _____

    _____

    _____

Management Signature: _____

Date: _____

Management's Title: _____

FIGURE 13D.5 Approved Write-Offs Compliance Form

Company Name: _____								
Compliance Testing						**Performed by:**_____		
Control Activity: Approval for Inventory Write-Offs								

Month Tested: _____

Item	Item Number	Amount	Description	Support Doc.	1	2	3	Exceptions

Attributes Tested:
1. Write-off amount trailed to the appropriate general ledger account
2. Write-off amount is listed on the "initialed as approved" Write-Off Report
3. Supporting documentation lists the same item number, description, and number of items

FIGURE 13D.6 Approved Write-Offs Testing Form

COMPLIANCE AUDIT PROGRAM Control Activity: Contract Procurement				
Item #	Procedure	Perf. by	Date	Comments
1.	Obtain list of contracts exceeding $25,000 for the current audit year			
2.	Obtain all supporting documentation regarding contracts subject to the competitive bidding process			
3.	Obtain updated Conflicts of Interest Form from all employees			
4.	Determine the following for each of the contracts: a) Evidence that all contracts exceeding $25,000 were approved by the board of directors b) Verify that bidding process regulations were followed for all contracts exceeding $25,000 c) Verify that there are no questionable connections between employees and contracts in excess of $25,000			

Management Response:

Were exceptions noted?   _____

If yes, document the response to these exceptions below:

Example: _____

_____

_____

_____

_____

_____

_____

Management Signature: _____

Date: _____

Management's Title: _____

FIGURE 13D.7   Contract Procurement Compliance Form

Company Name: _____

Compliance Testing   Performed by:_____

Control Activity: **Contract Procurement**

Year Tested: _____

Item	Contract Description	Final Cost	Vendor	Support Doc.	1	2	3	Exceptions

<u>Attributes Tested</u>:

1. Contracts over $25,000 were approved by the board of directors
2. All regulations related to the bidding process for contracts over $25,000 were followed
3. No questionable link can be made between company employees and contracted vendor

FIGURE 13D.8 Contract Procurement Compliance Testing Form

COMPLIANCE AUDIT PROGRAM Control Activity: Required Approval for Nonstandard Journal Entries				
Item # Procedure	Perf. by	Date	Comments
1. Obtain the printout of the Nonstandard Journal Entry Report			
2. Obtain the Journal Entry Vouchers for that month's non standard journal entries			
3. Trail Journal Entry Vouchers to the appropriate general ledger account			
4. Determine the following for each of the Journal Entry Vouchers: a) Evidence that the voucher has been initialed by the accounting supervisor, management, and the accounting clerk who posted b) All documentation supports the account and amount reflected on the voucher and in the general ledger c) All documentation was and is still attached to the voucher d) Evidence that the Journal Entry Voucher has been filed properly within the accounting department files			

Management Response:

    Were exceptions noted?   ——

    If yes, document the response to these exceptions below:

    Example: _____

    _____

    _____

    _____

    _____

Management Signature: _____

Date: _____

Management's Title: _____

FIGURE 13D.9   Approved Journal Entry Compliance Form

| Company Name: _____ | | | | | | | | | Performed by:_____ |

Compliance Testing

Control Activity: Approval for Nonstandard Journal Entries

Month Tested: _____

Item	Voucher Number	Account	Amount	Support Doc.	1	2	3	4	Exceptions

Attributes Tested:
1. Voucher has been initialed by the accounting supervisor, management, and posting clerk
2. Account and amount are the same between the general ledger and the voucher
3. All supporting documentation is still attached to the voucher
4. Journal Entry Voucher is filed properly within the accounting department files

FIGURE 13D.10 Approved Journal Entry Compliance Testing Form

COMPLIANCE AUDIT PROGRAM Control Activity: Master Vendor File Audit				
Item #	Procedure	Perf. by	Date	Comments
1.	Obtain the Master Vendor File			
2.	Obtain all supporting documentation regarding new vendors for the year			
3.	Determine the following for each: a) Evidence that all New Vendor Establishment Forms have been approved by management b) Verify that all confirmation and validation work from the original New Vendor form was originally completed c) Vendor file is properly filed with all supporting documentation			

Management Response:

    Were exceptions noted? _____

    If yes, document the response to these exceptions below:

    Example: _____

    _____

    _____

    _____

    _____

Management Signature: _____

Date: _____

Management's Title: _____

FIGURE 13D.11 Master Vendor File Compliance Form

Company Name: _____								Performed by: _____
Compliance Testing									
Control Activity: Master Vendor File Audit									
Year Tested: _____									

Item	Vendor ID	Name	Last Payment Date	Amount	1	2	3	Exceptions

Attributes Tested:

1. New Vendor Establishment form approved by management
2. All confirmation and validation work was properly completed on form
3. Vendor file is properly filed with all supporting documentation

FIGURE 13D.12   Master Vendor File Compliance Testing Form

	COMPLIANCE AUDIT PROGRAM **Control Activity: Authorized Check Signer Approval**			
Item #	Procedure	Perf. by	Date	Comments
1.	Obtain a list of disbursements for the current month			
2.	Select 20 disbursements from this list for compliance review			
3.	Obtain the supporting documentation for each of the selected disbursements			
4.	Determine the following for each of the selected disbursements: a) Check amount agrees to supporting documentation b) Documentation supports a valid business purpose c) Supporting documentation has been initialed by authorized check signer			

Management Response:

Were exceptions noted? _____

If yes, document the response to these exceptions below:

Example: _____

_____

_____

_____

_____

_____

_____

_____

Management Signature: _____

Date: _____

Management's Title: _____

FIGURE 13D.13 Authorized Check Signer Compliance Form

Company Name: _____
Compliance Testing   Performed by: _____
Control Activity: Authorized Check Signer Approval

Month Tested: _____

Disb #	Date	Amount	Payee	Support Doc.	1	2	3	Exceptions
1								
2								
3								
4								
5								
6								
7								
8								
9								
10								
11								
12								
13								
14								
15								
16								
17								
18								
19								
20								

Attributes Tested:
1. Check amount agrees to supporting documentation
2. Documentation supports a valid business purpose
3. Supporting documentation has been initialed by authorized check signer

FIGURE 13D.14   Authorized Check Signer Approval Compliance Testing Form

		Perf. by	Date	Comments
COMPLIANCE AUDIT PROGRAM **Control Activity: Large Disbursements Audit**				
Item #	Procedure			
1.	Obtain list of all disbursements exceeding $25,000 for the audit year			
2.	Obtain all supporting documentation regarding disbursements subject to the dual signature requirements			
3.	Obtain list of contracts subject to competitive bids for the audit year			
4.	Determine the following for each of the disbursements: a) Evidence that all disbursements exceeding $25,000 were dual signed by authorized check signers b) Verify that all documentation for large disbursements is authentic and properly filed c) Verify disbursements in excess of $25,000 that should have been subject to the bidding process were properly approved			

Management Response:

Were exceptions noted? _____

If yes, document the response to these exceptions below:

Example: _____

_____

_____

_____

_____

_____

_____

Management Signature: _____

Date: _____

Management's Title: _____

FIGURE 13D.15   Large Disbursements Compliance Form

Company Name:_____

Compliance Testing   Performed by: _____

Control Activity: Large Disbursements Audit

Year Tested: _____

Item	Disbursement Description	Amount	Vendor	Support Doc.	1	2	3	Exceptions
1								
2								
3								
4								
5								
6								
7								
8								
9								
10								
11								
12								
13								
14								
15								
16								
17								
18								
19								
20								

Attributes Tested:

1. Contracts over $25,000 were dual signed by authorized check signers
2. All supporting documentation is authentic and properly filed
3. All regulations related to the bidding process for contracts over $25,000 were followed

FIGURE 13D.16 Large Disbursements Compliance Testing Form

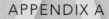

The Fraud Policy

 ## SAMPLE FRAUD POLICY*

Policy Statement

The {Board of Directors/Owners} of _____ are responsible for the prevention and detection of fraud. All parties should be familiar with the types of fraud that might occur and should be alert for any indication of fraud.

Scope

This policy applies equally to any fraudulent activity involving not only employees but also directors, vendors, outside agencies, and/or unknown parties, without regard to length of service, title/position, or relationship.

Actions Constituting Fraud

The terms *fraud*, *misappropriation*, and *irregularities* refer, but are not limited, to:

Any dishonest or fraudulent act
Forgery or alteration of documents

---

*Should not be adopted until reviewed and approved by company legal counsel.

Misapplication of funds or assets
Impropriety in reporting transactions
Profiting on insider knowledge
Gifts from vendors (outside of limits)
Destruction of records or assets
Disappearance of records or assets
Disclosure of confidential information
Any similar or related irregularity

Nonfraud Irregularities

Identification or allegations of personal improprieties or irregularities, whether moral or behavioral, should be resolved by departmental management, executive management, and/or the human resources department, rather than audit-related departments or agencies.

Reporting Structure (Tailor to Your Organization, e.g., Committee Reporting, External Fraud Hotline)

The {board of directors} of the organization has established a formal reporting mechanism whereby any individual who has knowledge of any suspected fraudulent activity can anonymously report these suspicions. Please reference the {Company Name} Fraud Reporting Policy for the proper reporting of suspicions. Any individual making a notification in accordance with the Fraud Reporting Policy is protected by the whistle-blower protection provisions of this fraud policy. In no circumstance should an individual confront the fraud suspect or attempt his/her own investigation.

Investigation Responsibilities

Upon receipt of the notification of alleged fraudulent activities, the {responsible parties as defined in the Fraud Reporting Policy} must investigate the specific allegations, utilizing available internal and/or external resources. The {responsible parties} shall retain in its possession all documentation regarding the nature of the allegations, the date the allegations were received, the resolution of the allegations, and the date resolved. Decisions to refer investigation results to the appropriate authorities for prosecution will be made in conjunction with legal counsel, the board of directors, and senior management.

Authorization for Investigation

Those individuals or agencies assigned the responsibility for investigation may take control of and gain full access to the organization's records and premises without prior consent of any individual who may have custody of any such records or facilities.

Acting in Good Faith

Any individual reporting any irregularity in accordance with the Fraud Reporting Policy must be acting in good faith and have reasonable grounds for believing the information provided. Allegations made maliciously or with knowledge of their falsity will not be tolerated. Individuals making such allegations may be subject to organizational disciplinary action and/or legal actions by the individuals accused of fraudulent conduct.

Whistle-Blower Protection

Employees may not retaliate against a whistle-blower for reporting an activity that person believes to be fraudulent or dishonest. Retaliation can be evidenced by the intent of adversely affecting the terms or conditions of employment (including, but not limited to, threats of physical harm, dismissal, transfer to an undesirable job assignment, demotion, suspension, or impact on salary or wages). The whistle-blower is defined as an employee who reports allegations of fraud in accordance with the provisions of the Fraud Reporting Policy. Whistle-blowers who believe that they have been retaliated against may file a written complaint with {responsible party such as corporate legal counsel}. Any complaint of retaliation will be promptly investigated by the {responsible party} and appropriate measures will be taken if allegations of retaliation are proven. This protection from retaliation is not intended to prohibit managers or supervisors from taking action, including disciplinary action, in the usual scope of their duties and based on valid performance-related factors.

Suspension/Termination

During an investigation, the suspected individual may be suspended with pay. Based upon the results of the investigation, the individual will either be reinstated or terminated under the direction of organizational legal counsel. Fraudulent activities will be prosecuted to the fullest extent of the law.

Acknowledgment and Signature

I have read the contents of this fraud policy. I understand that management will not tolerate fraudulent or dishonest activities of any kind and that I am not to engage in such acts while employed by _____.

_____

Signature

_____

Date

The Fraud Reporting Policy

SAMPLE FRAUD REPORTING POLICY*

Policy Statement

As referenced in the fraud policy of {Company Name}, the {responsible parties} have established this policy to provide a framework for reporting suspicions of fraud. {Company Name} commits to properly addressing the concerns of employees as submitted in accordance with the provisions of this policy.

Scope

It is understood that employees, directors, vendors, and other outside agencies may report suspicions of fraud under this policy. It is also understood that the scope of this policy can include reporting suspicions of fraudulent activity allegedly performed by employees, directors, vendors, or other outside agencies against the organization.

---

*Should not be adopted until reviewed and approved by company legal counsel.

Reportable Actions Constituting Fraud

The terms *fraud*, *misappropriation*, and *irregularities* are synonymous terms commonly used to refer to occupational or internal fraud. There are three types of fraud: asset misappropriation (the taking of company assets), corruption (collusion between at least two parties to gain personally while causing a loss to the company), and financial statement fraud (misrepresenting the financial position and/or results of operations).

Fraud can include, but is not limited to, any dishonest act, misapplication of funds or assets, profiting on insider knowledge, destruction of records or assets, disclosure of confidential information, forgery or alteration of documents, impropriety in reporting transactions, gifts from vendors (outside of limits), disappearance of records or assets, and/or any similar or related irregularity.

Predication (Reasonable Cause)

The Company has implemented this policy to encourage reporting suspicions that fraud is occurring or has been perpetrated against the organization. It is understood that in making a report in accordance with this policy, proof-positive evidence is not necessary. The potential reporter does not have to be right. The potential reporter should simply consider what predication, or reasonable cause, exists to make a report.

Accordingly, those considering making a report under this policy should provide some type of documentation that a fraud may have been committed or at least indicate that the specific issue may appear to be fraudulent in nature. It is the responsibility of the investigators to form the conclusion that presentable fraud has occurred. Maliciously false or frivolous reports made under this policy will be dealt with in accordance with the provisions noted in the fraud policy.

Reporting Mechanism

The {board of directors, owners} of the organization have established a formal reporting mechanism whereby any individual who has knowledge of any suspected fraudulent activity can anonymously report these suspicions. The reporting process is as follows: {the remainder of this section will provide the details of the selected processes of reporting}.

Notifications made in accordance with this policy will be handled according to the provisions of the Company's separate fraud policy.

Acknowledgment and Signature

I have read and understand the contents of this fraud reporting policy.

_____

Signature

_____

Date

Form FN-1

ANONYMOUS SUBMISSION OF ALLEGATIONS OF FRAUD

Date Submitted: _____   *Do NOT provide your name*

Submitted by: (Optional)

☐ Employee
☐ Customer/Member
☐ Vendor
☐ Other _____

Specific Allegation(s):

Please provide a description of the alleged fraudulent activity, including the suspected individual's(s') name(s) and position within the organization. Please attach any supporting documentation you might have regarding the alleged violation.

_____
_____
_____
_____
_____
_____

FIGURE B.1 Anonymous Submission of Allegations of Fraud, Form FN-1

The Expense Reimbursement Policy

 SAMPLE EXPENSE REIMBURSEMENT POLICY*

Policy Statement

It is the intent of the governing body of _____ to provide company-issued credit cards and/or bank account–related debit cards for official company use only.

Scope

This policy applies to any and all employed staff, owners, and/or members of the governing body and to any and all usage of the company-issued credit or debit cards and/or cash advances issued for company-related travel.

---

*Should not be adopted until reviewed and approved by company legal counsel.

Authorized Uses

Authorized uses of the company-issued credit or debit cards are as follows:

Travel Costs
Airfare
Lodging
Shuttle service
Rental vehicles
Gasoline for rental vehicles
Meals, documented as outlined in this policy

Purchases
Office supplies
Other expenses when the purchase order process is not available

Unauthorized Uses

Unauthorized uses are any personal charges whatsoever, including but not limited to personal meals, personal telephone usage, in-room movies, and in-room minibar usage detailed on hotel room bills.

Violations

The initial violation of the provisions of this policy will result in the removal of the privilege of use for a period of six months and a formal reprimand. Violations related to failure to provide supporting documentation will result in the charge being considered personal and thus subject to refund to the company. A second violation will result in termination.

Documentation

Receipts and Invoices

Receipts and invoices supporting cash and credit or debit card usage *must* accompany the monthly required expense report. The receipts or invoices should be attached to an 8½-by-11 piece of paper, which is then attached to the expense report. Sufficient description should be provided on the attachment to assist the accounting department in coding the charge to the proper general ledger account.

Supplemental Documentation for Business Meal and Entertainment Expense Charges

A separate supplemental business meal and entertainment charges form will be completed for each charge. This form requires additional documentation, as noted on the form.

All of these types of charges must be accompanied by original receipts attached to an 8½-by-11 piece of paper. Receipts must include *both* the itemized food and beverage receipt and the payment receipt (including gratuity).

The expense report form and, if applicable, the supplemental business meal and entertainment expense charges form must be submitted to and approved by the preparer's supervisor. Management's forms must be approved by the owner or a member of the board of directors.

Failure to follow these documentation requirements will result in the employee reimbursing the company for the charge.

Statement of Responsibility

The use of the company-issued credit or debit card is an important privilege that is intended to facilitate business by the company. Adherence to this policy is vital not only in ensuring the continuation of this privilege but also in ensuring that neither you nor the company is subjected to financial hardship or public criticism.

I, _____, have read and understand the responsibilities outlined in this policy. I agree to abide by the provisions in this policy and understand that violations of this policy could result in disciplinary actions, including termination.

_____

Signature

_____

Date

Month: _____   Employee: _____

Day	Payee	Lodging	Meals	Entertain-ment	Other Travel			Other Expense			Grand Total	Paid with	Receipt
					Description	GL Acct #	Amount	Description	GL Acct #	Amount			

General Ledger Account

Cash Advance _____
Cash Used _____

Due from Employee _____

Employee Signature _____   Approval Signature _____

Date _____   Date _____

FIGURE C.1 Expense Report Form

Payee: _____

Amount: _____

Classification: _____

Date: _____

Time: _____

Place: _____

Explanation of Business Purpose:

_____

_____

_____

_____

_____

_____

_____

_____

Name(s) of Attendee(s):

_____

_____

_____

_____

_____

Business Relationship between
Employee(s) and Guest(s):

_____

_____

_____

_____

_____

Verification of Responsible Employee Attendee: (Signature) _____

1. To be completed when charging or reimbursing for meal and entertainment expenses.

2. All expenses that are submitted must be accompanied by original receipts taped to an 8½-by-11 piece of paper. Receipts must include both the itemized food and beverage receipt and the payment receipt (including gratuity).

FIGURE C.2 Supplemental Business Meal and Entertainment Charges

APPENDIX D

Forms

Identified Fraud Risks and Schemes	Likelihood	Financial Significance	Risk Ref. No.

FIGURE D.1 Fraud Risk Assessment Framework Form

Company Name:
Anti-Fraud Program
Documentation of Control Activities
Date:

Control Activities
1
2
3
4
5
6
7
8
9
10
11
12
13
14
15

FIGURE D.2 Control Activities Documentation Form

Company Name: _____								
New Vendor Establishment								
Vendor Information		Validation Procedures Documents or Procedures Performed						
Vendor Name:								
Taxpayer ID#:								
Payee Name:								
Duplicate Name Search:								
Primary Phone:								
Fax No.:								
Website:								
Physical Address:								
Address:								
City:								
State:								
Zip Code:								
Mailing Address:								
Address:								
City:								
State:								
Zip Code:								
Duplicate Address Search:								
Contact Person:								
Contact E-mail:								
Expected Transactions:								

Vendor Relationships:

FIGURE D.3 New Vendor Establishment Form

COMPLIANCE AUDIT PROGRAM				
Control Activity: _____				
Item #	Procedure	Perf. by	Date	Comments
1.				
2.				
3.				
4.				
5.				
6.				
7.				

Management Response:

    Were exceptions noted?_____

    If yes, document the response to these exceptions below:

_____

_____

_____

_____

_____

_____

_____

_____

Management Signature: _____

Date: _____

Management's Title: _____

FIGURE D.4 Compliance Audit Program

Company Name: _____								Performed by: _____
Compliance Testing								
Control Activity: _____								
Month Tested: _____								

Item				Support Doc.	1	2	3	Exceptions

Attributes Tested:
  1.
  2.
  3.

FIGURE D.5   Compliance Audit Working Paper

SCOTCO, Inc.
Conflict of Interest Form

To be completed annually by all employees, owners, and members of the governing body. If there are any questions as to what category a relationship should be included, select one, and management shall determine any necessary reclassifications.

Name: _____

Title: _____   Signature: _____

Please provide individual names, company names, and the nature of the relationships that may exist with organizations that our company does business with or that you could reasonably expect our company to potentially enter into a relationship with, as relates to:

Family Relationships:

_____

_____

_____

_____

Personal Relationships:

_____

_____

_____

_____

Business Relationships:

_____

_____

_____

_____

Financial Relationships:

_____

_____

_____

_____

FIGURE D.6   Conflict of Interest Form

About the Author

Steve Dawson, CPA, CFE, is the founder and president of the Dawson Forensic Group of Lubbock, Texas. For over three decades, he has performed forensic investigations, internal control design consulting, accounting records reconstruction, litigation support services, and forensic training services for various agencies and industries located throughout the United States.

He began his career in 1984 serving on the audit staff at one of the nation's top 400 accounting firms, the Lubbock, Texas, auditing firm Bolinger, Segars, Gilbert & Moss. He became a partner of the firm in 1994, a position he held until his retirement in 2011. Mr. Dawson obtained his certified public accountant certificate in 1987 and his certified fraud examiner certificate in 2001.

Mr. Dawson has performed numerous forensic investigations and litigation support services for agencies such as the U.S. Securities and Exchange Commission (SEC), the Federal Deposit Insurance Corporation (FDIC), the National Credit Union Administration (NCUA), the Federal Bureau of Investigation, the Texas Rangers, and other local, state, and federal regulatory agencies. He also performs forensic services for private companies throughout the United States.

Upon his early retirement from Bolinger, Segars, Gilbert & Moss, he founded the Dawson Forensic Group for the sole purpose of combatting small business fraud through investigation, consulting, and training. With a passion for helping small businesses with their unique internal control issues, the Dawson Forensic Group opened the Institute for Small Business Internal Controls, which offers anti-fraud education and internal control design services.

He is a nationally recognized speaker in fraud detection, prevention, and internal control design methodologies. He is a graduate of Texas Tech University with a Bachelor of Science degree in Accounting and a member of the Association of Certified Fraud Examiners, the American Institute of CPAs, and the Texas Society of CPAs.

Mr. Dawson lives in Lubbock, Texas, with his wife, Ebeth, and enjoys spending time with their four grown children and grandchildren.

Index

Page numbers in *italics* refer to illustrations.